Association for Middle Level Education

Watching Students GLO

General Learner Outcomes build character and Career & College Readiness skills in the middle grades

Sandy Cameli, EdD

Printed in the United States of America.

ISBN 978-1-56090-279-9

Library of Congress Cataloging-in-Publication Data

Cameli, Sandy, 1950-

Watching students GLO : general learner outcomes build character and career & college readiness skills in the middle grades / Sandy Cameli, Ed.D.

pages cm

Includes bibliographical references and index.

1. Moral education (Middle school) 2. Life skills--Study and teaching (Middle school) 3. College preparation programs. I. Title.

LC268.C243 2015

370.11'4--dc23

2015025917

AMLE™

Association for Middle Level Education
4151 Executive Parkway, Suite 300
Westerville, Ohio 43081 | amle.org

Dedication and Acknowledgements

This book is dedicated to all educators tirelessly keeping the dream alive, by inspiring young adolescents to reach their fullest potentials through middle level structures and support. And, although others may not understand the passion and devotion for working with 10- to 15-year-olds—affectionately referred to as *walking hormones*—middle level teachers persevere with a common mission, vision, and drive that will forever make a difference in the field of education, as well as inspire the students they have the privilege of learning with on a daily basis.

Mahalo to the Hawai'i Department of Education, the Hawai'i Association of Middle Schools (HAMS), West Hawai'i Complex Area schools in Kailua Kona, Hawai'i, and the teachers of Konawaena Middle School in Kealakekua, Hawai'i—whom I've had the the extraordinary honor of working with over the years. I humbly share this resource as a tribute to your excellence as role models for the middle level profession!

Introduction

Middle level principles and tenets call for advocating for the developmental, social, emotional, physical and intellectual needs of young adolescents (Carnegie Council on Adolescent Development [CCAD] , 1989; Erb, 2001; National Middle School Association [NMSA], 1995, 2003, 2012). From advisory programs, teaming arrangements, and flexible groupings to interdisciplinary projects, block scheduling, and exploratory classes, schools that contain any combination of grades 5 through 8 have enhanced traditional schooling by providing foundational structures to support middle grades learners.

In *This We Believe: Keys to Educating Young Adolescents* (NMSA, 2010), the Association for Middle Level Education (formerly National Middle School Association) updated its mission for educating 10- through 15-year-olds to include "the 16 characteristics of successful schools." The 16 identified characteristics were categorized by curriculum, instruction, and assessment; leadership and organization; and culture and community. Successful middle schools also have four key essential attributes—they are developmentally responsive, challenging, empowering, and equitable. The framework lends itself to honoring the ongoing changes society, communities, and individuals experience while sustaining best practices in the field of education (NMSA, 2010).

Teachers familiar with the traditional 3Rs (reading, 'riting & 'rithmetic) often found content to be the driving force behind educational initiatives; whereas more modern twists introduced the 3Rs as rigor, relevance, and relationships that increase critical thinking and connectivity to the students' world. However, neither structure put the ownership for growth in the hands of the intended audience: the learner. The General Learner Outcomes (GLOs) used in Hawai'i's public school system (Hawai'i State Department of Education [HIDOE], 2013) are the foundational framework for instilling self-directedness into all students in grades K–12 as they navigate their current world of academia and prepare for future opportunities. The GLOs are lifelong learner skills appropriate for the *classroom, community,* and *career*—the 3Cs in an individual's life that provide a support structure for learning in and out of the classroom environment and enable students to customize skills applicable to their own lives.

This resource provides an overview of the GLOs, including applicability in the classroom, transference to community involvement, and beneficial structures for helping with character, college, and career paths. Specifics for implementing the teaching of these lifelong skills in advisory classes or any other classes are also included. Chapters four through nine provide classroom-tested activities for development of each skill as it is exhibited in the classroom, the community, and careers. Specific directions for teaching each activity and reproducible student handouts make these activities ones you can do tomorrow. And lastly, the book discusses the importance of student-led conferences in developing self-directed learners who can analyze and communicate their lifelong skills development.

The General Learner Outcomes (GLOs) have been used in advisory classes, core subjects, interdisciplinary projects, team activities, and as whole school themes to promote foundational skills for lifelong learners. Because the GLOs are foundational life and social skills, educators can incorporate them into any content, grade level, or learning structure. In subsequent chapters, lessons will be highlighted as individual GLOs or as all-inclusive traits; examples of individual, partner, team, and whole class activities will be shared; and reproducible masters are included in each chapter for classroom use.

Advisory is highlighted in this resource because it lays the groundwork for holistic support throughout a learner's day. The activities are non-graded and non-evaluative and are easily adapted to any skill or readiness level; teachers can differentiate as they see fit based on their classes and students.

Contents

Chapter One

Setting an example is not the main means of influencing another, it is the only means.

—Albert Einstein

What Are The GLOs?

In 2000, Hawai'i public schools introduced the General Learner Outcomes (GLOs) to complement academic programming with character development and lifelong skills curriculum for students. The six over-arching goals (HIDOE, 2013) are categorized as: (1) Self-Directed Learner, (2) Community Contributor, (3) Effective Communicator, (4) Complex Thinker, (5) Quality Producer, and (6) Effective and Ethical User of Technology. The curriculum provides student-friendly definitions of each trait to aid learners in understanding and aiming for proficiency of each. The GLOs are foundational supports incorporated across disciplines, grade levels, and learning environments allowing students many and diverse opportunities to practice using these tools.

Self-Directed Learner

Definition: Self-directed learners take responsibility for their own learning by managing timelines, monitoring progress, and self-assessing growth by reviewing strengths and areas for improvement.

Teacher actions: Teachers introduce the use of calendars, daily planners, or assignment logs. When teachers post upcoming homework assignments or projects, students record these same tasks, which helps them to complete requirements in a timely fashion. Additionally, instructors who help students set up personal record-logs in binders or tablets aid learners in monitoring their own work completion, missing assignments, or tasks to be redone.

Student actions: By using *I can* statements, students are able to articulate their ownership of responsibilities. For example: *I can develop plans for long-range goals* or *I can check on my progress and identify issues interfering with my learning.* In a nutshell, a self-directed learner is someone who takes care of his or her own responsibilities.

Community Contributor

Student-friendly definition: Although many students think simply working in a group without arguing exemplifies this trait, it involves breaking down how an individual effectively works on a team so that common outcomes are achieved by all. Community contributors have the ability to respect the feelings, ideas, abilities, and cultural differences of others while being cooperative and encouraging in-group situations.

Teacher actions: Team building activities, ideally introduced at the start of the school year, aid in promoting collaboration among peers in partner, team, and whole group activities. Likewise, establishing class norms with students support respectful expectations.

Student actions: Common phrases and self-talk that reinforce the standard and provide criteria to help students self-assess their contributions to a collaborative task or project are: *I use appropriate nonverbal cues and body language in my group* and *I consider others' point of view.* A successful community contributor is cognizant of his or her opinions or behaviors and how they may impact others and learns to think before speaking or acting. Working together respectfully is the foundation of community contributors.

Effective Communicator

Student-friendly definition: Many young adolescents may still perceive speaking as the sole means of communication, even though many are active digital communicators. Effective communicators possess the ability to listen, interpret, and use information appropriately in various forms for a variety of purposes and audiences. Through the written, spoken, electronic or non-verbal formats, communication etiquette and guidance are important for all learners.

Student actions: Students can self-assess their proficiency as effective communicators with statements such as: *I actively listen to others to gain a better understanding, I can pre-determine the best form of communication based on the purpose or audience for the task,* or *I am able to communicate my ideas clearly and without bias to others.* When a learner is able to understand the complexities and distinct characteristics of varying types of communication, he or she is better equipped to effectively convey ideas, as well as connect with others in a variety of situations and circumstances.

Complex Thinker

Student-friendly definition: A complex thinker is able to consider multiple perspectives, generate new and creative ideas, evaluate the effectiveness of his or her own creation or the work of others, and make necessary adjustments to challenges encountered. This trait encourages the pupil to seek wisdom and to strive for ownership of understanding, rather than just accepting an answer or explanation based on face value.

Teacher actions: Empowering students to reason and reflect enables learners to solve problems and analyze critical situations

Student actions: Complex thinkers evaluate their proficiency through *I can* statements like: *I can use prior knowledge to acquire new skills, I can apply creativity to problem solving,* and *I can apply critical analysis to evaluate a situation and change my point of view when presented with sufficient evidence.* The ability to deduce, debate, and/or determine validity of complex situations allows students to own their viewpoints while establishing credibility amongst peers and audiences.

Quality Producer

Student-friendly definition: A successful quality producer is a learner who has the ability to recognize and understand criteria set for quality performances and products. Quality can be defined by excellence, value, or worth depending upon the criteria established. And, at the school-level, many times the standards are pre-set by curriculum, programming or instructors. However, for students to rise to the expectation of becoming quality producers, they must first understand the expectations for final products or outcomes.

Teacher actions: Teaching skills such as rough drafts and peer-conferencing to make sure all tasks are completed and proper steps followed before turning in an assignment for final assessment will enable students to acquire this trait. The ability to pause and reflect before simply checking off a job from the *To Do List* is paramount for middle level learners.

Student actions: An individual who understands stipulated expectations is able to verbalize his or her understanding: *I can describe criteria necessary for a project or assignment, I understand the skills necessary to produce a quality task,* or *I use feedback to improve my work.*

Effective and Ethical User of Technology

Student-friendly definition: Effective use of technology includes proper handling and care of equipment while in use; whereas ethical practices involve appropriate use of school-level tools for legitimate tasks. An effective and ethical user of technology is able to use a variety of technologies to produce an idea or product; use technologies to access and manage information; understand the impact technology has on individuals, family, society, and the environment; use technology appropriately for communication, collaboration, research, creativity, and problem solving; and understand and respect legal and ethical issues related to technology.

Teacher actions: Frequent reminders, with unambiguous samples, are important tools to include when teaching students about efficacy and principled expectations of technology use. As societal and education-related expectations change regarding technology inclusion in the classroom, so must the requirements and safeguards put in place to guide and protect its users. The ultimate outcome is for all users to be mindful while utilizing such a powerful resource.

Student actions: Students exhibiting effective and ethical standards are able to state: *I can access and manage online information responsibly, I can organize and communicate data through spreadsheets and databases, I know how to cite and document sources,* and *I understand the legal and ethical issues related to technology.*

Introducing the GLOs

As students begin the school year, advisory teachers often use class time to kick-start student thinking about the GLOs and how the traits can be practiced across the curriculum. Activities can include

- Brainstorming sessions of the six GLOs around table teams.
- *Anatomy of a GLO-ing Student* for individuals to personalize mini-posters of themselves exhibiting said traits (see p. 8).
- Once students have begun dialoging about the GLOs, a non-graded quiz (see pp. 10–11) will help them verbalize and coin phrases aligned to specific GLOs. When students and teachers are speaking the same language, consistency of expectations increases.
- Games, class challenges, and hands-on projects can also build understanding and regular use of characteristics within the GLOs.

Anatomy of a GLO-ing Student

Target: To help students identify GLO attributes within themselves through a creative outlet.

Objectives:
(Students will:)

- Independently identify at least six traits (one for each GLO) that he/she practices/utilizes on a regular basis
- Decorate a paper doll/template to resemble his/her physical features, clothing, and personality
- Label the paper likeness with the GLO attributes

Materials:

- "Anatomy of a Student" worksheet
- Markers, colored pencils, crayons, assorted art supplies

Steps:

1. The teacher reviews GLOs, asking students to share examples demonstrated in school; the class brainstorms ideas and discusses them.
2. Using "Anatomy of a Student" worksheets, the students create personal likenesses of themselves with labels indicating GLOs demonstrated in/outside of school. The teacher encourages them to make drafts/sketches before finalizing mini-posters.
3. Sharing as whole class, in small groups, or in partners; classes may also want to post display on bulletin board or students can keep the results in binders/tablets as a reference for future use.

WORKSHEET

Anatomy of a Student

Personalize this drawing to represent you & how you use the GLOs!

Non-Graded GLO Quiz

Target: To identify criteria and descriptors specifically aligned to each of the six General Learner Outcomes (GLOs)

Objectives:
(Students will:)

- Independently self-assess knowledge of the six GLOs
- Collaborate with peers to discuss alignment of criteria to specific GLOs
- Engage in friendly debates with peers regarding criteria alignment

Materials:

- "GLO Quiz" worksheet
- Colored pencils

Steps:

1. The teacher explains that students will be taking a non-graded quiz as a self-assessment. Distribute handouts, give students time to complete.
2. In partner pairs, students compare results with each other. Students place a plus next to questions the partners share in common, and a question mark next to differences in answers.
3. Ask partners to join another duo to form a team of four. The team now compares their results as a four-some. Using a different colored pencil use the same system of pluses or question marks to indicate similarities and differences. As the team discusses the reasons that each criteria belongs aligned to a particular GLO, students can agree or respectfully disagree.
4. As a whole class discussion, the teacher reads each GLO statement one by one encouraging table teams to share their answers along with how their team came to their decision or multiple perspectives. The goal is not to assume correct or right answers exist, but rather give learners the opportunity to better understand properties associated with each GLO.

Optional: Students can opt to post tallies next to each GLO statement as a whole class overview of perception data.

Worksheet

Name: ______________________ Date: ______________ Class Period: _____

General Learner Outcomes (GLOs) Quiz

Directions: Match the descriptions of successful student examples to each GLO. They will be used more than once.

(A) Self-Directed Learner
(B) Community Contributor
(C) Complex Thinker
(D) Quality Producer
(E) Effective Communicator
(F) Effective/Ethical User of Technology

__________ I know how to share jobs and responsibilities when I am on a team.

__________ I put time and effort into my work to produce quality assignments.

__________ I show creativity and originality when designing projects.

__________ I can set goals, keep track of them, and reflect on my successes.

__________ I understand the importance of an Acceptable Use Policy with computers.

__________ I listen, interpret, and use information effectively for a variety of purposes.

__________ I am respectful of feelings, ideas, and abilities of others in my group.

__________ I respect the legal and ethical issues related to technology.

__________ I am responsible for my own learning and can monitor my progress.

__________ I can select a topic to study and expand upon it considering multiple perspectives.

__________ I recognize quality products and understand criteria necessary to meet requirements.

__________ I can communicate appropriately for the correct audience and purpose.

__________ I am able to generate new ideas and evaluate their effectiveness.

__________ I have the ability to produce quality evidence to meet or exceed the standards.

__________ I manage my time and resources effectively to meet goals.

__________ I respect cultural differences of peers by inviting their opinions during group discussions.

Teacher key for quiz

General Learner Outcomes (GLOs) Quiz

Directions: Match the descriptions of successful student examples to each GLO. They will be used more than once.

(A) Self-Directed Learner
(B) Community Contributor
(C) Complex Thinker
(D) Quality Producer
(E) Effective Communicator
(F) Effective/Ethical User of Technology

B I know how to share jobs and responsibilities when I am on a team.

D I put time and effort into my work to produce quality assignments.

C I show creativity and originality when designing projects.

A I can set goals, keep track of them, and reflect on my successes.

F I understand the importance of an Acceptable Use Policy with computers.

E I listen, interpret, and use information effectively for a variety of purposes.

B I am respectful of feelings, ideas, and abilities of others in my group.

F I respect the legal and ethical issues related to technology.

A I am responsible for my own learning and can monitor my progress.

C I can select a topic to study and expand upon it considering multiple perspectives.

D I recognize quality products and understand criteria necessary to meet requirements.

E I can communicate appropriately for the correct audience and purpose.

C I am able to generate new ideas and evaluate their effectiveness.

D I have the ability to produce quality evidence to meet or exceed the standards.

A I manage my time and resources effectively to meet goals.

B I respect cultural differences of peers by inviting their opinions during group discussions.

Chapter TWO

I feel that luck is preparation meeting opportunity.

—Oprah Winfrey

Supporting the Classroom, Community, and Careers

Because the General Learner Outcomes (GLOs) are so fundamental and have long-lasting impact on the growth and development of successful citizens, they became the over arching goals for Hawai'i's public school standards-based curriculum (HIDOE, 2013). Dr. Martin Luther King, Jr. proclaimed, "Intelligence plus character—that is the true goal of education" (King, n.d.). Schools strictly focusing on academics minus the social, emotional, developmental, and disposition of students often find graduates ill-equipped to navigate challenges in the real world. Learners introduced to the GLOs during their elementary years—and reinforced in the middle grades—are prepared to incorporate these traits in high school and post-secondary arenas more successfully.

Classroom Practices

As with most effective learning practices, variety is the spice of life. The GLO examples included in this chapter work with whole classes, small groups, partner pairs, and individuals, depending on the focus of the lesson. The teacher, through mini-lessons, often introduces whole class activities at the start of a unit. Class discussions, interactive games, and service-learning projects are samples of just how GLOs can be used for whole group learning. Table teams and small groups provide a more personal approach to understanding the GLOs as students work together to complete tasks. When learners use the GLOs to design posters, develop scripts for skits, or sponsor school-wide initiatives, they take ownership of their own growth as well as pride in showcasing skills to others.

Whether a student chooses to work with a peer through partner pairs, or individually, a more purposeful effort can be placed on GLO understanding through originality. Independent ideas can manifest themselves through creative writing (i.e., poetry, stories, and comics), technology-based projects, oral presentations, and reflections.

Table Team Scenario (Activity 3): Ms. Masukawa asks her seventh graders to create life-size paper dolls to represent the "mean-est" student in the school in order to reinforce math-averaging skills. Small groups of 4 or 5 students collect data from peers on height, eye and hair color, shoe size, birthdates, favorite clothing brands, and other interesting demographics related to today's teen. The classroom is buzzing with activity and chatter as students gather statistics to design their paper peer and prepare to share with others. Upon conclusion of the activity, the teacher asks students how GLOs were used in this activity, and to back up answers with evidence. Comments range from, "We were definitely *community contributors* since everyone had a role to complete", "*Effective communication* was used in our group and when we had to present to the class", and "I think Annie—our paper peer—shows *quality* since we drafted her first on scratch paper, and planned out how to represent her on the larger poster paper".

Rather than using the GLOs as an add-on or expecting students to complete extra work to support their overall learner growth, this teacher infused the GLOs as a natural part of daily conversations and classroom expectations.

Community Impact

Although they are not familiar vernacular to many stakeholders of a school, GLOs can be naturally incorporated into a community's practice and expectations for effective citizenship. Many of the activities described in this resource will bridge classroom application to real world and community involvement.

Learners transitioning to college-level settings may find the GLOs a natural fit as they continue to use skills acquired in their K–12 experiences. However, a more sophisticated use of the skills needs to be applied to post-secondary degrees. Goal setting for program requirements allows high school graduates to be self-directed; partner with peers for lab sessions for collaborative skills; effectively show proficiency through report and composition writing; use critical thinking skills to resolve challenging scenarios; continue to draft, revise, and fulfill tasks in order to master requirements; and exhibit efficacy and ethics in the use of technology-validating competencies.

Likewise, in career and workplace-related environments, employers expect workers to take initiative independently (self-directed); collaborate with clients, colleagues, and supervisors (community contributor); use oral and written communication effectively (effective communicator); use ingenuity and problem-solving skills (complex thinker); show effort, high standards, and pride in work (quality producer); and demonstrate successful and principled usage of technology (effective and ethical use of technology).

College applications and job descriptions are beginning to include skills (similar to GLOs) in advertisements and expectations for applicants. Students able to understand, use, and master said skills have an advantage over fellow candidates who may not possess the full complement of traits.

> **Service Learning Scenario (Activity 4):** In Ms. Goeas' eighth grade classroom students are eager to suggest community outreach projects, but many do not have the resources to implement all of the ideas. Most, however, understand the concept of struggle since many of the families in their own community survive on state assistance and free or reduced lunch status. During one of their brainstorming sessions, a humble young lady mentioned how her family would shop at the local thrift store each year to purchase gifts for others, and even though prices were considerably reduced, the expectation to shop during the holidays was a burden and added undue stress to her parents. Through more discussion the class offers to create its own holiday thrift store for the community in which no money would change hands, but rather donations would come in from volunteers and businesses willing to help. Families could shop using tokens created by the students to provide gifts for the holidays. Student helpers would also be available to provide free gift wrapping after participants completed their shopping.
>
> Upon completing the service project, Ms. Goeas asks students to reflect on the success of the activity as well as the GLOs used during the experience. Sentiments include: "We were stuck in the beginning about the money-thing, but once we came up with the token system it all fell into place—I think that shows *complex thinking*!" "Many of us were *self-directed* when we talked to businesses about our project and gathered donations", "We also used *technology* to create the flyers and share our goals with others through social media".

The community outreach shared by these students broadened their perspectives of the interdependence of individuals, resources, and experiences. Additionally, the opportunity for students to own their ideas, actions, and philanthropy became a powerful incentive for future goals.

Career Connection

An important facet to understanding, practicing, and modeling the GLOs is the connection a learner makes between present and future applications. The common mantra "When will I ever use this?" is answered when classrooms begin to show relevant connections to learners' future scenarios. Many students remember being asked as a 5-year-old what they wanted to be when they grew up, but few recall inquiries like "How will you be a self-directed learner when you are 20?" or "Can you share the type of complex thinking you will be using as the CEO of a company when you're 30?" Most children would be confused or scared off by those questions, yet these are skills needed for their future paths.

Teachers can use skills introduced in the lesson today to springboard a student's thinking toward future scenarios. Goal setting is just one of the ways teachers plant the seed in learners to envision their futures.

> **Goal Setting Scenario (Activity 5):** During a weekly advisory class, Mr. Gambone asks his sixth graders to close their eyes for an experiment. Amongst giggles and one-eyed peekers, the majority of the class complies. "Envision your house 20 years from now. What does it look like and where will you be living?" He invites students to share while keeping their eyes closed. Various responses from beachfront cottages to mansions in the sky begin to arise. "Now, imagine the types of clothes you will be wearing?" Hands are raised and elaborate designs are shared. "Dresses will be out of foil, and shoes will have tiny, little jets that allow us to float!" one girl offers as the class erupts in laughter. Smiling, the teacher continues, "Ok, ok", reining the class back in, "How about your job? What type of career will you have or work will you be doing?" Initially quiet, and pausing for thought, the class thoughtfully ponders the question, as evidenced by the furrowed brows around the room.
>
> A boy raises his hand and offers, "I guess I'll work construction like my dad." A second voice shares, "I want to go to college, but I'm not sure how my family will get money for that, so I'll probably stay here and work at a store." A third volunteer pipes in, "I might not know what I want to do for a job, but I definitely know I don't want to be a teacher—they have to put up with brats like us!" Once again laughter fills the room, with a grinning instructor, but the seed has been planted in these students' minds regarding their future.
>
> "One more", the teacher challenges, "What does an employer/boss imagine the perfect employee looks or acts like?" Again, the class pauses, but soon offers ideas, "They come to work on time", "Someone who does their work without being told", "Somebody who can answer the phone politely", and "A person who gets along with the customers or other people in the business". The teacher nods, as he knows the students are primed for the activity.
>
> After the class discussion, Mr. Gambone has students create past, present, and future timelines extending to the students' 30th birthday. Each child notes highlights from their childhood and current accomplishments during middle school. Plans for high school are

> penciled in, and goals for post-secondary intentions are labeled on the timeline. Above notable benchmarks, GLO qualities are listed to indicate which skills helped to make (or will make) the event a success. One 11-year-old girl labeled *Effective Communicator* and *Self-Directed Learner* above her win at the school-wide spelling bee; a boy at a neighboring desk added *Effective Use of Technology* next to family vacation video for his grandmother's 75th birthday—the student created an iMovie to capture the family's highlights; and, twin soccer stars in the class noted *Community Contributor* skills helped them on and off the playing field to get along with each other. By creating these visuals, students have reference points and targets to remind them of their life trajectories.

The above scenario promotes imagination and prediction skills while helping to guide students toward realistic goals. When students are able to see the GLOs as foundational skills for success in life, they are more likely to incorporate them seamlessly into recurring rituals and routines.

The GLOs serve as a basis for including character-related traits into a school's instructional programming, by way of interdisciplinary means. Results from students, staff, parents, and community members accepting the GLOs as an integral part of a school's culture can support learners in the *here and now*, as well as the *yet to come*.

The Mean-est Student

Target: The goal of this lesson is for students to understand the concepts of mean, mode, and median through the use of data collected from peers reflecting on the characteristics of today's teen.

Objectives:
(Students will:)

- Develop viable questions for collecting data about student interest
- Interview classmates with questions designed to gather statistics on students' height, eye color, shoe size, birthdates, clothing preferences
- Combine data with their peer group to determine averages of data collected
- Create a pseudo-student representing the mean (average) of peers' data
- Identify GLOs associated with this activity

Materials:

- "The Mean-est Student" worksheet
- Banner/poster paper
- Markers, colored pencils, assorted art supplies

Steps:

1. Review the concepts of mean, mode, and median prior to this lesson; also, provide instructions on viable questions for data collecting.
2. Day 1: Working in teams of four or five, students review questioning techniques appropriate for data collection and divide responsibilities for collecting the data. They brainstorm questions related to peer interest (physical characteristics, music, clothing, foods).
3. Day 2: Students bring collected data from questions to class and share with teammates. Groups work to determine averages of characteristics and favorites of the typical teenager. On banner paper groups draw life-size paper-peers; they decorate and label them to indicate the *mean*-est student in class. Students display paper-peers in the classroom and discuss how the data gathering determined their final projects.
4. The teacher concludes the lesson with a discussion of the GLOs and how they were used in all stages of the project.

Worksheet

Name: ______________________ Date: ______________ Class Period: ______

The Mean-est Student

Your individual tasks:

- Develop five questions to ask peers regarding clothing, physical features, ages/birthdates, favorites, etc.
- Collect data on at least 10 seventh graders on campus, based on questions developed.
- Determine which GLOs were necessary/used to complete tasks.

Your group's tasks: (4–5 members)

- Compile all data into a group's database; determine mean, mode, and median of data collected.
- Based on data gathered, sketch a draft of your "paper-peer" that represents ***mean***-est qualities.
- Create a life-size poster version of the "Mean-est Student" to be shared with the class.
- Discuss and be prepared to explain which GLOs were used and how they contributed to this project.

Assessment based on completion of the following:

- Questions created reflect characteristics of a seventh grader.
- Data collected from 40–50 sources and compiled to determine averages.
- Creation of a "paper-peer" to represent the mean-est student at school.
- Presentation to class to include steps, strategies, and GLOs used.
- Self-reflection of contributions made and outcomes gained.

Service-Learning Plan

Target: To understand the processes and steps involved in planning an event or activity that benefits the school, community, or a large group of participants.

Objectives:
(Students will:)

- Use the process of brainstorming and collaboration for decision-making purposes
- Design, prepare, and implement a service-learning plan through philanthropic means
- Self-assess and reflect on outcomes

Materials:

- "Service-Learning Plan" worksheet
- Additional materials to be determined by project design

Steps:

1. The teacher opens class with a discussion of service-related projects completed by past classes.
2. The whole class brainstorms suggestions for a new service project. The class lists ideas on the board; teams of students form to work on different aspects of the project.
3. Individual students use "Service-Learning Plan" to brainstorm ideas for their portion of the project. Team members divide responsibilities among themselves, and draft timelines, and benchmark tasks to keep on target to meet requirements.
4. At various stages of the project, students share which GLOs they are using and how people are benefiting from students' exhibiting GLOs.

Worksheet

Name: ______________________________ Date: ______________ Class Period: ______

Group: ____

Service-Learning Plan

My Responsibilities:

Timeline & Goals:

Task/Date:
Task/Date:
Task/Date:
Task/Date:

Groups' Responsibilities:

GLO-ing Timeline

Target: The goal of this lesson is for students to utilize a timeline to predict future events in their lives based on past and present activities, as well as future goals.

Objectives:
(Students will:)

- Identify events from their elementary years that demonstrate GLOs
- Label current activities from middle school that demonstrate GLOs
- Make predictions for high school and post-secondary events that will align with the GLOs
- Create a visual timeline of events and GLOs from birth to age 30

Materials:

- "GLO-ing Timelines" worksheet
- Poster paper and markers/colored pencils (optional)

Steps:

1. The teacher holds a class discussion with students about their futures. Students make predictions about houses, clothing, pop culture and careers. The teacher specifically asks students to envision their own jobs and professions, and what types of skills will be necessary to be successful. With suggestions provided from students, the teacher asks students to identify which GLOs each career will require and to give specific examples.
2. The teacher hands out "GLO-ing Timelines" worksheet (and asks students to chart significant events from their childhood and elementary years, followed by current middle school activities. Finally, students make predictions for high school and career opportunities that students set as goals. Above each event, students code GLOs that were developed or used during each significant activity.

Optional: Students use the "GLO-ing Timelines" worksheet and final timelines completed on poster paper to make classroom displays.

worksheet

Name: ______________________________ Age: ________

Birthdate: ______________ Place of Birth: ______________________

GLO-ing Timeline

Tasks:

1. Create a timeline highlighting events from your elementary and middle school years.
2. Predict plans and/or events for your high school and adult years to age 30.
3. Label GLOs as they have helped you accomplish tasks/events, and how they will help you achieve future goals.

Codes:

SDL = Self-Directed Learner; **CC** = Community Contributor; **EC** = Effective Communicator; **CT** = Complex Thinker; **QP** = Quality Producer; **EEUT** = Effective & Ethical User of Technology

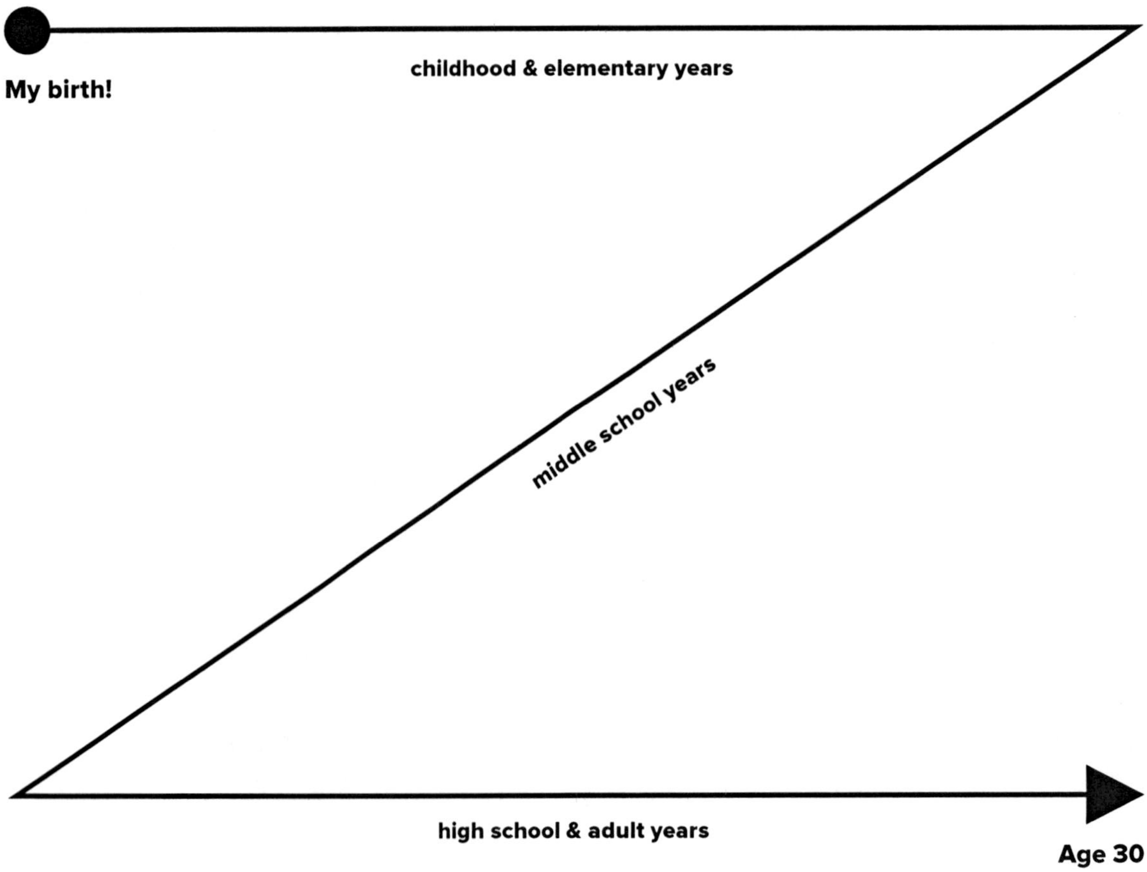

Chapter Three

Humility is not thinking less of yourself,
it's thinking of yourself less.

—C.S. Lewis

Creating a GLO-ing Advisory

Advisory is one of the foundational tenets of middle level programming. An advisory class is not a homeroom, study hall, or content-specific course; it is a smaller, supportive environment geared to providing guidance, team building, collaboration, and service-learning opportunities for young adolescents (CCAD, 1989; NMSA, 1995; Wormeli, 2001). Designed to provide an advocate for every child on campus, advisory time supports moral and character development of middle level learners (Erb, 2001; Jackson & Davis, 2000; NMSA, 2010). And, in alignment with college, career, and character readiness, the GLOs are a natural fit through advisory for introducing and reinforcing lifelong learner skills (HIDOE, 2012).

Although it is a fundamental structure for middle schools, advisory is not uniform in appearance or practice, as it works best when customized for a school's unique needs and programming. In one Hawai'i middle school, students start the day and end the day in advisory class, spending approximately 30 minutes each school day with an adult advocate and a smaller group of peers. Activities align with the six GLOs and help learners transfer these life skills to content area classes on a daily basis. For example, to promote each GLO, the following rituals and routines are practiced:

Self-Directed Learner: use of daily planner and calendaring of projects/events.

Community Contributor: use of TRIBES© or Kagan© strategies (Kagan, 2013) to promote cooperative learning (CenterSource Systems, 2014).

Effective Communicator: prepare for student-led conferences and portfolios.

Complex Thinker: use problem solving tasks and brain-teasers to promote critical thinking.

Quality Producer: introduce and review how rubrics and scoring guides are used for assessment purposes.

Effective and Ethical User of Technology: review of school's Authorized User Policy (AUP) for Technology and administration of Internet Driver's License.

Although non-evaluative in nature, advisory practices and programming reinforce skills that transfer to content-specific courses, and have been proven to show an increase in student achievement when routinely utilized. Additionally, schools employing regular advisory periods have noted decreases in absenteeism, behavioral issues, and learner disengagement (Brody, Shulkind, & Foote, 2009).

The following vignettes offer a glimpse into advisory classes using GLOs effectively:

> **A New School Year:** With new backpacks in tow, and tentative smiles appearing, Mrs. Onaka's class eagerly anticipates the start of the new school year. These students came in from self-contained elementary classes and will now follow a routine of six separate class periods along with six different sets of expectations, timelines, and requirements. To prepare these learners, the teacher must establish rituals and routines immediately and reinforce practices on a daily basis.
>
> The sixth graders receive student planners on the first day of school and learn how to fill in assignments for each class in corresponding days. Starting from Day 1, Mrs. Onaka circulates the room initialing or stamping each child's planner as evidence that assignments were recorded accurately. This reinforces the habit for each learner and provides verification for parents and family members monitoring daily tasks or upcoming projects, tests, and events.
>
> By the third week of the school year, most students have adopted the routine and the teacher spot-checks planners on a weekly, rather than daily basis, transitioning students from dependent to independent *Self-Directed Learners.*
>
> **Working Together:** Holidays at the middle level can often increase excitability levels, off-task behaviors, and distractions for students; thus, proactive teachers employ cooperative strategies while channeling excess energy into productive activities through advisory. In Mr. Pieronek's class, the upcoming holiday door decorating contest, sponsored by the Student Leadership Council, provides the perfect opportunity for students to practice collaboration while focusing on a service-learning component. Based on the theme "A Season for Giving", teachers encourage classes to decorate a classroom door, which will remain on display through the month of December. Top prize will be a monetary gift to be donated to a charity of the winning class' choice.

Pieronek's seventh graders are anxious to participate, and confidently proclaim their winning status, even before the competition begins; however, they have no plan or idea of how to start. The opportunity to guide the students through brainstorming, shared decision-making, planning and execution of tasks, and completion of goals is a recipe for success in this advisory class. Using principles of teamwork (paired partners, triads, quad groups and whole class) the variety of groupings allow students to hear ideas from various perspectives. Providing job descriptions and applications for different roles allows for a more even playing field, rather than the standard first-come, first-serve approach; and, modeling best practices of teamwork reinforces expectations the teacher has for effective collaboration. All steps assist students in honing their *Community Contributor* skills, which benefit the advisory as well as content-based classes.

Using Communication Journals: Typically, young adolescents equate communication with verbal forms solely and often neglect the power of the written word, which is why daily journal prompts prove to be successful vehicles for supporting *Effective Communicators* in Mrs. Rom's advisory. Building on essential rituals and routines for middle level learners, sixth graders in Mrs. Rom's class expect to see a quote, prompt, or question on the board when they enter the room each morning. Equipped with marble-style tablets designated for advisory activities, students await the official start of the school day by pondering the statement presented. And, although the expectation is to record the prompt in their daily journal, learners may elect to discuss the topic with a neighbor, table group, or silently reflect through written form. Even without recording personal thoughts in the tablet, students may simply indicate "Discussed with partner" or "Debated with team" as evidence of participation in task. At the end of the school day, students revisit the same prompt and are asked if their opinion has changed based on new learning experiences throughout the school day. Once again, learners are given the option of communicating orally or in written form. The tablets are left in the classroom for the next day's topic, and Mrs. Rom spot checks them approximately once per week giving anecdotal feedback. The intention of the journals is to boost communication skills rather than for assessment purposes.

A Day at a Glance: Developmentally, young adolescents are concrete thinkers. Many struggle with abstract reasoning, and are reluctant to take risks due to teacher-pleasing conditioning experiences at the elementary level. As a way of supporting *Complex Thinkers*, Mrs. Apina challenges her eighth graders to stretch their cognitive skills through weekly brain teasers and problem solving tasks. One example may be to survive the entire day in school without using the pronoun "I". Students keep tally marks in their binders or notebooks of each time they forget, and bring the results to the end-of-the-day advisory class. A class discussion ensues regarding how an individual's perception changes when he or she is not allowed to think from the 1st person stance, but rather craft language and communication around 2nd and 3rd person formats. Another week, the challenge may be to seek out items, events, or actions from every letter of the alphabet and prepare to share what was identified at the end of the day. Finally, a quick check review of any day's activities invites students to play the 3-word game. In exit-pass fashion, as students prepare to leave school, Mrs. Apina asks learners to share three words that sum up learning or experiences of the day. Nouns, verbs, adjectives, and adverbs count—but must be aligned with the school day. Again, these non-threatening experiments allow students to rethink how learners analyze a day at a glance.

Encouraging Excellence: Quality is not instinctual for young adolescents, nor should it be assumed by teachers to be a natural trait of learners. Mr. Palakiko understands that, and purposefully builds *Quality Producer* opportunities into his seventh grade advisory class in order to support students in all content areas. By using the acronym SUPER, students are able to review assignments and projects before turning in for assessment or evaluation purposes.

> ***S*** = Steps followed – Have all stages of the process been followed?
>
> ***U*** = Understand expectations – Do you know what the final outcomes are?
>
> ***P*** = Parts included – Have all parts and pieces been included in task?
>
> ***E*** = Eye-catching – Is work neat, organized, and easy to read/understand?
>
> ***R*** = Read to turn in – Have all previous steps been reviewed and completed?

Mr. Palakiko introduces students to the format at the start of the school year and continues to refer to the various steps for daily assignments, weekly tasks, and performance-based projects. The structure enables students to adopt a process, which allows learners to take responsibility for their own learning, as well as future opportunities.

GLOing Ambassadors: To capitalize on the plugged-in generation, Ms. Gunnarson tasks her eighth graders with supporting all GLOs through technology. Growing *Effective and Ethical Users of Technology* requires exposure and experience in order to support navigating ever-changing online environments. Early in the school year, after all six GLOs have been reviewed in advisory classes, Ms. Gunnarson breaks students into sub-groups that correspond with each GLO. Learners are tasked with proposing technology supports for each area. The Complex Thinker team may generate a list of apps and rate each (Ex: Luminosity) for peers to download on mobile devices; the Effective Communicator group may offer to demonstrate the use of a website or online tool that assists students in argumentative writing skills. Students in Ms. Gunnarson's advisory have the option of sharing their resource bank with other advisories or grade levels to support the school as a whole via a GLOing Ambassador program. The opportunity for students to own their learning experiences through personal investment is powerful and benefits more than just the individual learner.

Advisory can be a catalyst for school-wide initiatives and thematic programming. Its foundation is grounded in best practices for the whole child during the pivotal years of early adolescence (NMSA, 1985). And, although preparation for successful advisory activities can add time to a busy teacher's schedule, the long-term effects and affects are invaluable, and ultimately impact learners' social, emotional, developmental, and academic achievement throughout their middle school years. Middle level educators willing to invest time, energy, and resources into advisory programming will find other structures within the school naturally compliment the process and reap benefits from such an overarching investment.

Chapter Four

Intelligence plus character—that is the goal of true education.

—Martin Luther King, Jr.

How to Grow a Self-Directed Learner

Learning to learn, taking initiative, and independently owning one's progress is not only vital to success in the classroom, but also imperative for an individual's future plans. Self-directed learners are not usually born, but are grown through guidance, modeling, and practice. According to Thomas Carruthers (n.d.), educational theorist, "A teacher is one who makes himself progressively unnecessary." Lessons in this chapter provide opportunities for students to learn to function independently in the classroom and community and prepare students to be self-sufficient and autonomous in their future careers.

Classroom Example

> **Tri-fold Terminology (Activity 6):** Allows students to understand the role and responsibilities of the self-directed learner, and because the focus of this first GLO is on the self, students perform the activity independently with a bit of classroom conversation.

While processing the terminology of "self-directed learner," the students also associate practices with meaning. The activity reinforces that self-directed learners set their own goals.

Community Example

Students often fail to assume there is a connection between what they learn in the classroom and their lives outside of it. They also often have trouble communicating with their parents what has happened in the classroom. Bridging the classroom-real life gap and classroom-home gap can help reinforce self-direction skills.

Learning interviewing skills and questioning techniques (Activity 7): Students must focus on what the "real" questions are, critically think about the purpose(s) of their pursuit of information, develop listening skills, and analyze how to reach different audiences.

Career Example

With money and time for training at a premium, employers highly value potential employees with self-direction skills. It is crucial that students enter adulthood adequately prepared to organize and plan their work, track important dates, and manage their time.

A Classified Approach to Self-Direction (Activity 8): Gives students real-world practice in relating the elements of self-direction to a career, experience, or volunteer opportunity.

Tri-fold Terminology

Target: The goal of this activity is to build vocabulary and understanding of the term *self-directed learner.*

Objectives:
(Students will:)

- Build vocabulary through synonym brainstorming and categorizing
- Work independently and in small teams to increase vocabulary terms
- Create visual representations of terminology

Materials

- Sticky notes
- "Tri-fold Terminology" worksheet
- Markers, colored pencils, crayons, assorted art supplies

Steps:

1. Teacher introduces the term *self-directed learner* by labeling each part separately in three columns (self, directed, learner) on the board or chart paper.
2. Students write synonyms for each column on three sticky notes and post them on the chart. The teacher facilitates a class discussion regarding similarities, differences, and insights of the suggestions.
3. Students use the "Tri-fold Terminology" worksheet to create a synonym for *self-directed learner* from the class list developed or using their own ideas. Once the students have filled in the text portion, the teacher encourages them to create visual cues or representations aligned with each column.
4. After completing all sections of the sheet, students cut out the rectangular shape and fold into thirds, taping to secure. The final products are displayed on desks or hung around the classroom.

worksheet

Name: ______________________ Date: ______________ Class Period: ______

Tri-fold Terminology

Directions: List words/synonyms that match the word at the top of the column. Draw/sketch a symbol or icon that represents the word to you at the bottom of the column. Add color or decorations to display. Cut outer box, then fold to create a 3-dimensional prism, secure with tape or glue.

Cut along outer box

(fold line) (fold line)

Self	Directed	Learner

Self-Direction Dialogs

Target: The goal of this activity is to teach students how to develop suitable questions for interviewing an adult about *self-direction*.

Objectives: (Students will:)

- Participate in a class discussion regarding interviewing protocol
- Draft ideas for questions aligned to topic
- Practice interviewing a peer based on questions developed
- Set date, time, and location for a formal interview
- Collect responses from interviewee based on questions developed

Materials:

- "Self-Direction Dialogs" worksheets
- Markers, colored pencils, crayons, assorted art supplies

Steps:

1. The teacher asks the students to reflect on effective interview questions: *What is the purpose? What are the components of an interview? How will the information be used?, How do you avoid questions that allow yes and no responses? And, will there be any follow-up conversations?* Class discusses questions.
2. The teacher reviews the term self-directed learner. Students predict how self-direction is used on a daily basis outside of school. The teacher asks students to think about an adult family member, neighbor, or coach who they might interview for this assignment.
3. In groups of 3 or 4, students draft questions about self-direction. The teams brainstorm queries and create a chart to share with classmates. Groups share out and add to a master list of questions generated by the whole class.
4. Using the "Self-Direction Dialogs" sheet and the master list of questions, students determine which questions they will use in their own interviews. Students hold practice sessions with peers, and they make final preparations to conduct a formal interview with their selected adult.
5. Independently, learners conduct the interview and collect responses. Upon returning to class, students share their experiences, answers, and insights.

Worksheet

Self-Direction Dialogs

Planning Stage:

Interviewer: ______________________ Interviewee: ______________________

Explain why this person was selected to interview: ______________________

____

____

____

Sample Questions:

Questions should be designed to help you understand how this person has used self-direction in their life.

Q1: ______________________

Q2: ______________________

Q3: ______________________

Q4: ______________________

Q5: ______________________

Q6: ______________________

Practice Stage:

Rehearse the interview with a classmate or friend; record responses below. This practice round will help you decide if any of the questions need to be altered before the actual interview.

Responses/answers:

Q1: ______________________

Q2: ______________________

Q3: ______________________

Q4: ______________________

Q5: ______________________

Q6: ______________________

Self-Direction Dialogs–Page 2

Interviewer: ______________________ Interviewee: ______________________

Revision Stage:

Will changes be made to any of the questions? If "yes", explain changes; if "no", explain what worked well with existing questions: ______________________

Preparation Stage:

Date of interview: ______________ Location: ______________________

Notes/answers gathered during interview:

Q1: ______________________

Q2: ______________________

Q3: ______________________

Q4: ______________________

Q5: ______________________

Q6: ______________________

A Classified Approach to Self-Directed Learning (SDL)

Target:

The goal of this activity is to help learners envision self-directed skills needed in college, career, or community environments.

Objectives:
(Students will:)

- Translate student-directed terminology into user-friendly language
- Discuss SDL skills as they apply to future opportunities
- Create an advertisement for a real world position using SDL terms

Materials:

- "A Classified Approach to SDL" worksheet
- Markers, colored pencils, assorted art supplies

Steps:

1. The teacher introduces the concept of classified ads or postings. Similar to texting or tweeting, the announcement needs to be clear and concise for readers to understand.
2. The class reviews characteristics of a self-directed learner and discusses which attributes will benefit individuals as adults.
3. The teacher distributes and reviews instructions for "A Classified Approach to SDL" worksheet. The teacher encourages students to create their own ad and corresponding translation related to a position they hope to acquire upon completing high school.
4. Students share orally and/or post in the classroom their completed sheets for others to build awareness of SDL skills in the real world.

A Classified Approach to SDL

Directions:

1. Participate in class discussion about self-direction in real world settings. What skills are you learning now that can be applied to your future opportunities?
2. Read sample and translation.
3. Generate your own classified ad for a position you hope to fill one day. Keep post short, but focus on self-directed skills necessary to be successful in role advertised.

   Complete an ad and translation at the bottom of this worksheet—continue on back of sheet if necessary. Use humor and creativity to get your message across to readers.
4. Share final product.

Sample Ad:

Job Opening: Our company is looking for a team player with strong time management skills, and the ability to monitor own progress without direct supervision. If you are interested in learning new skills with the possibility of advancement opportunities check out our website: self.directed.learner.com to complete an application.

Translation: Our company is looking for a **team player** *(someone able to work well with others)* with **strong time management skills** *(comes to work on time & is productive during their hours on the job)*, and the ability to **monitor own progress without direct supervision** *(sets goals and works toward to completing goals without being told what to do)*. If you are **interested in learning new skills** *(takes initiative to improve self)* with the possibility of advancement opportunities check out our website to apply.

Name: ______________________ Date: ______________ Class Period: ______

A Classified Approach to SDL–Page 2

Classified Ad:

____

____

____

____

____

____

____

____

Translation:

____

____

____

____

____

____

____

____

Chapter Five

Alone we can do so little, together we can do so much.

—Helen Keller

How to Grow a Community Contributor

The ability to communicate, collaborate, and consider others' contributions is not necessarily an innate skill or characteristic possessed by all students; thus, it becomes crucial for educators to provide opportunities for learners to hone these traits as they transition between classroom, community, and career. This chapter uses the *Classroom, Community,* and *Career* format to showcase lessons that build and strengthen community contributor-type skills for the middle level audience.

Classroom Example

Students greatly benefit from experiencing regular, frequent illustration or models of appropriate interactions between partners, teams, or groups in and out of the classroom. And, simply arranging desks or tables in collaborative formats does not guarantee automatic alliances or mutual respect amongst participants.

> **GLO-ing Governance (Activity 9):** Reinforces the fundamentals of equity in sharing and respectful listening. Students establish class norms or shared expectations early in the school year resulting in optimal results in achieving academic, social, emotional, and physical development.

Community Example

Often the language and lessons learned in school are not the same as those outside the classroom. This can add confusion to students' perception of *what happens at school, stays at school* syndrome. To help learners best articulate what the GLOs mean in their everyday lives, give them opportunities to share exemplars with families and community members on a regular basis.

In some communities, local newspapers will run "GLO Students of the Month" highlights, or participating merchants may offer tokens and treats of appreciation for students who receive recognition for exhibiting GLO qualities. These examples are some options that show support for the social, emotional, and developmental growth of the learner, as opposed to focusing solely on academics or athleticism. However, students need to understand how information is shared between the school and the community in order to appreciate the connections between the two.

One idea to try in the classroom focuses on writing, so this activity works best if students work with a single partner. The teacher begins by explaining the role of a town crier during medieval times as a way of spreading messages throughout the community or town. Messages had to be succinct but effective and understood by the masses.

For this task, the teacher would challenge students with composing a piece of writing that highlights and explains the GLOs to a community audience base. Ideas to heighten awareness of the GLOs may include

- A 30-second radio spot
- A 500-word overview in the local newspaper's "Community Corner"
- A 10-part Q&A for an online blog
- A submission to the school's parent/family newsletter
- A creative writing option proposed by the student to the teacher

Based on the time of school year, grade level of students, and writing proficiencies, teachers decide the time frame that best meets the needs of the learners as well as how final products will be shared.

Career Example

As with many activities conducted in the classroom or at the school level, learners often struggle to find relevance to personal, community, or real world connections. Thus, it becomes essential for teachers to help find missing links to bridge the gaps in understanding and application. Appealing to students' future plans and interests will elicit fascination and enthusiasm for activities proposed.

> **GLO-ing Careers (Activity 10):** Requires students to work in partner pairs or trios to align GLOs to jobs and occupations they perceive necessary for future careers.

Learning how to be an effective Community Contributor at the middle level also means preparing to carry these skills into high school and post-secondary arenas. Current societal rules expect individuals to know how to communicate with others, share ideas, collaborate on tasks, and pool resources for the greater good. If young adolescents are unable to practice and experience these skills or develop the appropriate attributes that allow them to demonstrate efficacy in cooperative situations, they are more apt to struggle to reach their full potential in contributing to society as an adult.

GLO-ing Governance

Target: The goal of this lesson is to help learners understand and identify criteria necessary for developing class norms and/or expectations.

Objectives:
(Students will:)

- Collaborate with peers to prioritize examples of acceptable behaviors and attitudes aligned to the General Learner Outcomes (GLOs)
- Create a list of possible classroom norms based on the GLOs to share with the class
- Participate in a gallery walk of group posters to vote for favorite choices to be used for establishing class norms
- Participate in a consensus exercise to adopt GLOs as classroom norms

Materials:

- "GLO-ing Governance" worksheet for each table team
- Poster paper and markers for students
- Colored adhesive dots or stickers

Steps:

1. Ask students to bring "Anatomy of a GLO-ing Student" to class. Working in groups of four, students take turns sharing results from their "Anatomy" sheets. Preface group discussions with two expectations: (1) There will be equity in voice/sharing by all; and (2) Listeners will be respectful during sharing.
2. After all sharing, teacher passes out "GLO-ing Governance" worksheet to each table team. Groups prioritize examples shared from peers to create a collaborative team set of GLO examples. The expectation is that everyone in the group contributes ideas/ examples to the worksheet.

GLO-ing Governance–cont.

Steps:

3. Based on the completed worksheet, the table groups create a poster version of the six GLO samples offered during the group discussion. After the poster is completed, the group hangs it in front of the classroom.
4. The teacher passes out six colored adhesive dots/stickers to each student. The class participates in a gallery walk reviewing all posters created and displayed by peer groups. Students use stickers to select/vote for the sample that exemplifies each GLO. After all learners have voted, the class analyzes the data collected to determine which examples or criteria were most popular per GLO. A discussion is held to determine if the highly rated examples would make for good guidelines and expectations in the classroom. A final list is generated and posted in the classroom as a reference; smaller versions are created for students to keep in their binders/folders.

Worksheet

Teammates: ______________________________

____

GLO-ing Governance

Directions:

- You will need your "Anatomy of a Student" worksheet as a reference
- Take turns sharing examples from each GLO
- Select the strongest evidence from each person's sheet to create a list of GLO samples below
- Select a spokesperson from your group to share your results with the class

GLO-ing Examples:

Self-Directed Learner: ______________________________

____

Community Contributor: ______________________________

____

Effective Communicator: ______________________________

____

Complex Thinker: ______________________________

____

Quality Producer: ______________________________

____

Effective & Ethical User of Technology: ______________________________

____

____

GLO-ing Careers

Target: The goal of this lesson is to help learners understand and identify criteria necessary for success in a profession or career based on the GLOs.

Objectives:
(Students will:)

- Collaborate with peers to develop criteria based on GLOs to align with a career
- Discuss attributes necessary to be successful in a selected career/job posting
- Design a visual representation of the career/job/profession by integrating GLOs into the artwork
- Students share with classmates by discussing the process and final product

Materials:

- "GLO-ing Career" worksheet for each table team
- Poster paper and markers or colored pencils for students

Steps:

1. In a class discussion, ask students to describe what types of skills a construction worker needs (any profession can be used). Chart responses. After multiple suggestions have been given, ask students to categorize the criteria—use colored markers to help the class visualize. Once suggestions have been grouped, ask students if they see any connections between the categories and the GLOs. Which GLOs are missing? How would a construction worker use all six of the GLOs?

GLO-ing Careers–cont.

Steps:

2. Pass out the "GLO-ing Careers" worksheet–One sheet per partner or trio. Explain to students they will be selecting a profession from a job posting for this activity. Students may use newspaper classified ads, online job postings, or employment offices to find a position. The task is to describe as many characteristics and attributes related to the GLOs necessary to be successful in this career choice.

3. Groups are then challenged to design a visual representation of the career/profession using the GLO traits determined in the project. Creativity is encouraged as these projects will be shared and displayed for others to view. Ideas will be abundant, but if learners need starting point ideas consider: a fire truck with six windows, each open space filled with criteria for successful use of the GLOs as a fire fighter; a bakery counter decorated with assorted desserts and pastries each filled with GLO examples for use by a pastry chef; or the night sky filled with planets, stars, and asteroids, each highlighting necessary attributes for astronomers.

Worksheet

Partners: ______________________________ Date: ______________

Profession/Career: ______________________________ Class Period: ______

GLO-ing Careers

Self-Directed Learner	Community Contributor	Effective Communicator
• ____________ • ____________ • ____________	• ____________ • ____________ • ____________	• ____________ • ____________ • ____________
Quality Producer	**Complex Thinker**	**Effective/Ethical User of Technology**
• ____________ • ____________ • ____________	• ____________ • ____________ • ____________	• ____________ • ____________ • ____________

Attach copy of employment ad here.

Chapter Six

The more elaborate our means of communication, the less we communicate.

—Joseph Priestley

How to Grow an Effective Communicator

Communication can be defined as the ability to convey or exchange thoughts, opinions, and knowledge by way of speech, written form, body language, or signals. Yet many middle grades students hear the word *communicate* and assume its association with speech only. Therefore, to support the growth of an effective communicator the classroom and school environment must provide awareness of the various modes of communication that students are constantly using to send messages and how their messages impact others. Lifelong learners need finely tuned skills to connect with and transfer information to others. Written and oral communication opportunities offered in tandem allow students to understand the benefits and dependency of each upon the other. Finally, middle grades students need varying scenarios and settings in which they can practice listening, speaking, writing, and conveying their messages to partners, table teams, and large groups to enhance their abilities to effectively communicate.

Classroom Example

Although students arrive in our classrooms able to speak, write, and share ideas, they often need structures in which refinement opportunities exist. Thus, ice-breakers or anticipatory set activities introducing a concept are great ways to ease into practices that can sometimes feel threatening to inexperienced communicators.

> **Give GLO, Get GLO (Activity 11):** The teacher asks students to think about what forms of communication exist or how we communicate with each other. Although learners will be tempted to share immediately, the teacher asks them to hold ideas until the activity begins. The teacher passes out the "Give GLO, Get GLO" worksheet (p. 66) and asks students to place two of their ideas in any of the boxes. Next, the teacher asks learners to interact with others in the room to collect other ideas and responses in empty boxes on the grid. The teacher encourages students

to fill as many boxes as possible from as many different people as possible within a given time frame. Upon completing the task, students share completed grids with a partner comparing and contrasting, even filling in any empty spots with new ideas.

During a class discussion the class charts common ideas categorized by writing, speaking, listening, and body language. Students indicate which examples on their individual grids they are comfortable doing by using symbols: ☺ = comfortable, ☹ = uncomfortable, ? = unsure.

Using the bottom half of the worksheet, students set goals based on areas they are unsure (?) or uncomfortable with (☹) to improve proficiency as an Effective Communicator.

The Give GLO, Get GLO activity blends oral communication with written snippets and goal setting in order for students to understand the importance of balancing all forms of communication in their academic and personal lives.

Community Example

The old adage, "Children are to be seen, but not heard," has definitely been updated to include student voice and expression through a variety of communication avenues. Most adolescents are adept with technology as digital natives and have little or no discomfort when it comes to personal sharing via texts or social media. However, along with innovation must come the understanding of limits and longevity when public access is involved.

Communities have expanded to include a flat world concept (Friedman, 2005) in which those who interact no longer need to attend the same school, live in the same neighborhood, or even shop at the same stores. A community now consists of anyone with similar interests, beliefs, and practices regardless of the continent on which one resides. Therefore, communication customs may or may not be the same for a middle schooler in Hawai'i as they are for a pre-teen in Pennsylvania or a young adolescent in Amsterdam. It is essential for educators to grow effective communicators for 21st century learners who have expanded their repertoire of communication environments and opportunities.

Effective Communication for e-Communities (Activity 12): The teacher posts the phrase *Lost in Translation* on the board, chart paper, or screen. Students brainstorm what the phrase means by deliberating with partners or table groups. Next, the teacher posts a second phrase "*A bat was used to hit the ball.*" When asked what the statement means, most students will reference the game of baseball. However, if the synonyms for *bat* and *ball* are replaced with images of a flying mammal and an elaborate social dance event, the translation takes on a whole new meaning. While the latter idea is sure to produce fits of laughter, the point of the lesson is to examine how intent of communication can be misrepresented innocently or deliberately.

The teacher then hands out the sheet "Effective Communication for e-Communities" (p. 68) to students. Learners are tasked with editing and providing solutions for scenarios depicted to insure the clearest of messages are conveyed for various audiences. A class discussion should include reminders of *netiquette*, etiquette for using the Internet, and protocol used when communicating through online or electronic means. Completed sheets can be displayed or saved for future reference.

Career Example

Middle level learners, so immersed in their ever-changing present, often struggle with the concept of how their present actions could impact their futures. They are familiar with phrases like, "*Sticks and stones may break my bones, but words will never hurt me*", or "*Actions speak louder than words*", as mantras to navigate social structures. However, how often do students think about the long-term or residual effects of messages gone bad from their pre-adult years? It is imperative for students to reflect and apply decision-making skills to a variety of communication formats in order to grow into an effective communicator.

Purple Pete and the Power of Words (Activity 13): The teacher begins class by asking students to think about how words or phrases can hurt someone if language is not a thing or an object. Learners brainstorm responses and share with partners, table teams, or the whole group. The teacher asks students to think about the apology *I'm sorry.* In spite of its being the accepted response by society, do the words remedy the harm of hurtful language as delivered? The aim of the lesson is for students to build empathy by connecting their words and actions to others' interpretations and feelings.

Using the "Purple Pete" worksheet (p. 71), students think of hurtful words or phrases they have used or heard used to insult others (Ex: You are stupid, you're a moron, dog-breath smells better than you do!) *Note: vulgar, obscene, or offensive language is unacceptable in this activity.*

Individually, each student will speak to Purple Pete using some of the insults and tearing a portion of the paper doll with each hurtful phrase used. For example: A student may say *Your clothes are ridiculous, Pete*—then tear off his left foot; or, *I hate the way you walk*—and tear off his right hand. Students should insult Pete 4–6 times and tear a piece of his body each time.

After the insulting and tearing is complete the teacher will ask students to repair Pete with tape, putting him back together as closely as possible. Each time a portion of Pete is reattached, a student expresses a compliment or apology. At the end of the activity, the teacher asks students to look at their Pete and reflect on his condition.

Although he has been reassembled, is he the same? Do the tears represent scars that will follow him through life? How can communication delivered early in one's life impact his or her future personalities or interactions with others? The teacher holds a reflective discussion with students and asks learners to express how the activity impacted their thinking about negative and positive communication.

Effective communication is an essential skill for middle grades students as they learn to balance written, verbal, whole body, and electronic formats for communicating. Students are exposed to various forms of connecting with, conversing about, and conveying information through home, school, community, and multimedia structures. Thus, it becomes imperative for learning environments to include opportunities for young adolescents to hone their communication skills effectively.

Give GLO, Get GLO

Target: The goal of this activity is for students to expand their understanding of communication in its various forms.

Objectives: (Students will:)

- Brainstorm a list of different forms of communication
- Interact with others to share and collect information
- Determine areas of growth to set goals for improvement

Materials:

- "Give GLO, Get GLO" worksheet
- Chart paper and markers

Steps:

1. The teacher asks students to think of various forms of communication and record two of their ideas in boxes of the grid on the "Give GLO, Get GLO" worksheet. Students interact and circulate around the classroom, sharing ideas with peers and gathering new information to fill their own grids.
2. A class discussion is held to share the collection of ideas gathered by all students. The teacher charts responses in categories (oral, written, listening, body language) on the board or poster.
3. Based on individual grids, learners are asked to label examples with codes corresponding to their comfort level of each activity: (Comfortable = ☺, Uncomfortable = ☹, Unsure = ?)
4. Students select two activities from the "Uncomfortable" or "Unsure" categories to set goals. Using the "Give GLO, Get GLO" worksheet, students create short-term and long-term goals. Short-term goals can be daily or weekly; while long-term goals can be set for monthly, quarterly, or semester ranges.

Optional: Teachers and students can decide if rewards or incentives will be awarded for goals achieved during specific time periods.

Worksheet

Name: ________________________ Date: ______________ Class Period: ______

Give GLO, Get GLO

Directions: Fill in two boxes with your own ideas, then interact with others to gather additional and/or new information until your boxes are all filled up!

Next Steps: Select two areas from boxes above that you want to set as goals for improvement. Fill in steps to show how you will reach your goals.

Short-term Goal #1 ________________________________

Long-term Goal #1 ________________________________

Short-term Goal #2 ________________________________

Long-term Goal #2 ________________________________

Short-term Goal #3 ________________________________

Long-term Goal #3 ________________________________

Effective Communication for e-Communities

Target: The goal of this activity is for students to understand the importance of clear communication in electronic formats.

Objectives:
(Students will:)

- Understand the phrase *lost in translation*
- Interact with others to share and collect information
- Evaluate phrases in text and online posts that can have dual meanings

Materials:

- "Effective Communication for e-Communities" worksheet
- Chart paper, markers, assorted art supplies

Steps:

1. The teacher begins by posting the phrase *lost in translation* on the board. Students discuss its meaning and any experiences they have had with the terminology. Next, a new phrase *A bat was used to hit the ball* is posted. The teacher asks students to explain its meaning. Most learners will reference a baseball game. By changing the synonyms for *bat* and *ball*, the teacher shows how the phrase could mean a flying mammal crashes into a social dance event.
2. A class discussion reveals other mistakes often made through communication in oral, written, or electronic formats. The term *netiquette* is introduced as a guideline for appropriate communication online. The class proposes expectations that could prevent "lost in translation" situations from occurring.
3. Using the worksheet "Effective Communication for e-Communities", students review samples and share suggestions with partners, table groups, or the whole class.

Optional: Students create and share "Dos & Don'ts" for netiquette or other electronic communication formats.

Worksheet

Name: ______________________ Date: ____________ Class Period: ____

Effective Communication for e-Communities

Sample text message *DF2 B Ben & Jer 2 party!*	Sample online post *Did you see Jessica's outfit? It looks cool!*	Create your own text or online post
What does this text likely mean? *Don't forget to bring friends Benjamin and Jennie to party!*	What does this post likely mean? *The writer likes Jessica's outfit and thinks it's a popular trend.*	What does this text likely mean?
What could this text mean? *Don't forget to bring "Ben & Jerry's Ice Cream" to party!*	What could this post mean? *Perhaps Jessica is traveling during winter and the weather is chilly-she could be bundled up.*	What could this mean?
How could this mix up or loss in translation create a problem?	How could this mix up or loss in translation create a problem?	How could this mix up or loss in translation create a problem?
Suggest a solution to communication issue:	Suggest a solution to communication issue:	Suggest a solution to communication issue:

Purple Pete and the Power of Words

Target:

The goal of this activity is for students to understand the importance of verbal communication and the impact it can have on individuals.

Objectives:
(Students will:)

- Discuss words and phrases that bring about emotional reactions
- Reflect on the phrase *I'm sorry* and its intent
- Participate in a simulation of cause and effect related to verbal communication and emotional reactions

Materials:

- "Purple Pete and the Power of Words" worksheet duplicated on purple paper
- Scissors and clear adhesive tape

Steps:

1. Students discuss with partners, table groups, or the whole class how words or phrases can hurt someone if language is not a tangible thing or object.
2. Students debate the pros and cons of the effectiveness of apologies and of the phrase *I'm sorry.*

Purple Pete and the Power of Words–cont.

Steps:

4. After students cut out Pete from the page so each learner has his or her own paper doll, the teacher explains that students will be talking to Pete, independently, and insulting him with hurtful words and phrases. Examples: *You are stupid or your breath smells like a dog's*. ***(Note: no vulgar, offensive, or obscene language may be used)*** Each time a harmful phrase is used, the students tear a part of Pete off. Example: If a student said, *Pete, I think your clothes are ridiculous*, then the student would rip off an arm or leg. Students insult Pete four to six times and each time they tear a piece of him off
5. After damaging the Pete doll, the students repair him one piece at a time with tape, and with each repair issue an apology or positive comment until he has been put back together
6. The class reflects on their "Petes" and discusses how even when reassembled, Pete will never be the same. The teacher poses probing, reflective questions such as: *Do the tears represent scars that will follow him through life? How can negative communication received early in life impact an Individual's interaction with others? How difficult was it to insult and rip Pete apart? How difficult was it to reassemble him? How will this lesson impact your communication with others?*

Purple Pete and the Power of Words

Directions: Cut Purple Pete out of this page before beginning the activity.

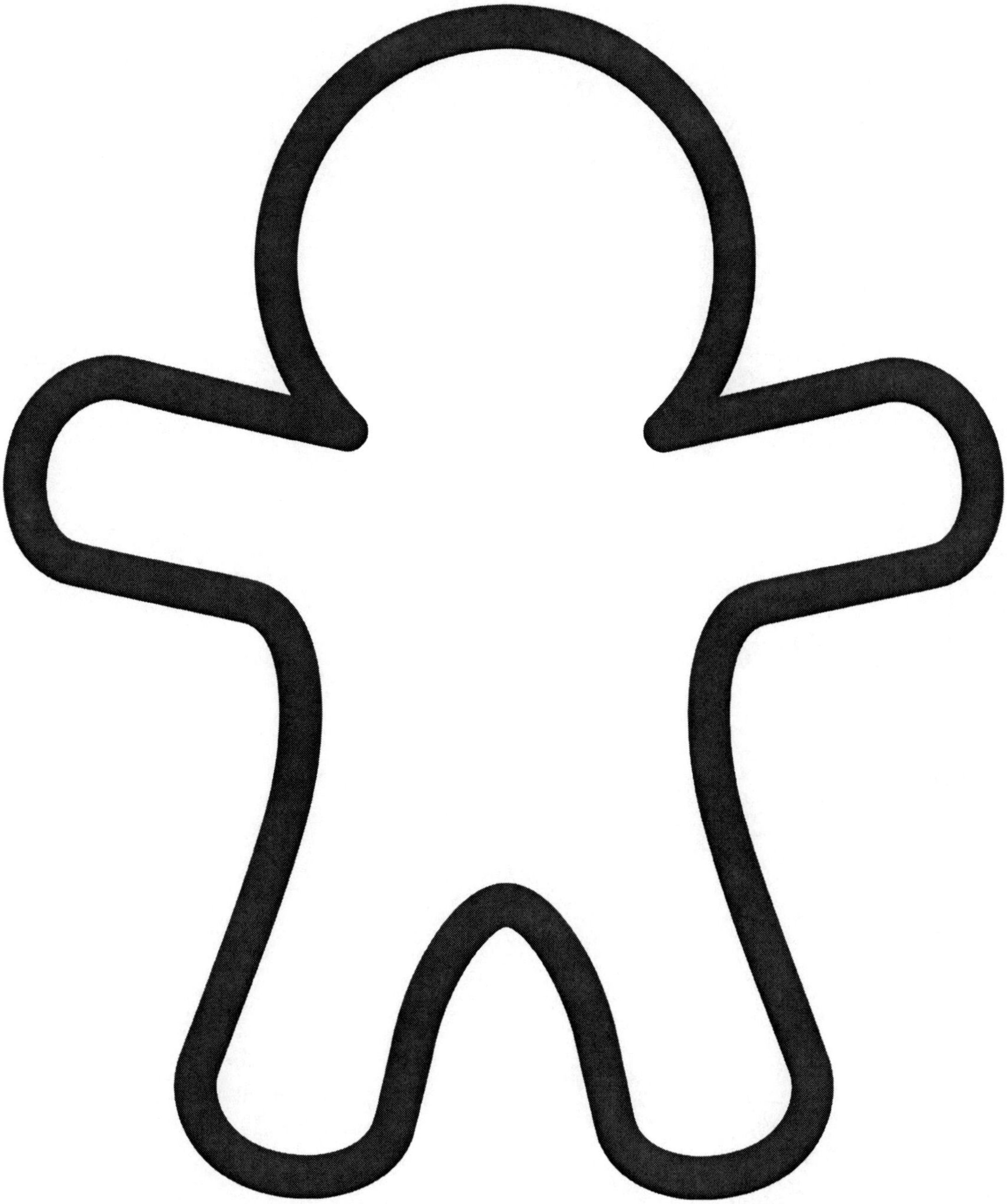

Chapter seven

I use my mind to solve problems
and invent.

—Temple Grandin

How to Grow a Complex Thinker

Complex thinking involves the ability to demonstrate critical reasoning and problem solving strategies in various situations, while considering multiple perspectives and viewpoints regarding challenges and obstacles. Complex thinkers additionally possess the capability to generate new and creative ideas through effective evaluation, and use ethical consideration to make adjustments as necessary to circumstances involving decision making.

Traditional school systems often create barriers that cause students to struggle in reaching their potential as complex thinkers. In right vs. wrong, one-size-fits-all, answer-factory classrooms, learners hesitate to take chances in practicing new skills, sharing original ideas, or thinking outside-the-box. In early adolescence, when risk-taking and non-conformity can translate to social suicide, middle schoolers can be reluctant to venture far from the comfort levels of norms or status-quo. Activities that best support complex thinkers include those that allow learners to

- Draw from previous experiences
- Reflect on viewpoints other than their own
- Apply non-conventional approaches to scenarios
- Evaluate the effectiveness of their decision-making to determine what changes or adaptations to make

Once students are equipped with tools that support reasoning, the sophistication of their thinking and awareness of future possibilities increases.

Classroom Example

Understanding another person's perspective or ideas can be difficult for adults, let alone students who are focused on the here and now and perpetuating the "Me" generation.

So, middle grades students need practice evaluating whether they are successfully transmitting the intent of their messages. The following activity allows partners to practice giving succinct directions for a complex task and then assessing outcomes by both participants.

> **Tell Me How, Show Me Now (Activity 14):** Allows students to experience the nuances of communication as they work in pairs (one the Giver, one the Receiver) with one partner having to draw a simple object only by listening to stated directions from their partner and with no visuals. After partner two completes drawing, the duo examines how accurate the pictures match by comparing the Giver's examples to the Receiver's sketches. The class discusses how different perceptions are associated with the same image or task and generates solutions and ideas to tackle future tasks in which shared perceptions are necessary in learning and working environments.

Community Example

Civic groups, legislative bodies, and volunteer groups commonly use problem solving at the community level. Service-learning opportunities abound for students to solve environmental or social issues in their neighborhoods. However, prior to learners diving into project planning, practice with problem solving of real world issues is necessary.

> **Woulda, Coulda, Shoulda (Activity 15):** Requires students to discuss pros and cons for solving actual scenarios that could occur in their own community. Learners reflect on three aspects of the scenario depicted: What *would* be done if the event happened in our own community? What *could* be done to prevent the future event? and What *should* be done to educate others about potential harm to the community? Students pose solutions to the problem depicted in the "What Would You Do?" show while proposing preventable options to be shared with family members, the neighborhood, organizations, and community members.

Career Example

Devising opportunities for young adolescents to practice problem solving that will apply to their future lives often results in activities in which students generate grandiose ideas and suggestions. However, middle grades students must practice and develop these critical skills if they are to be effective contributors to their families and communities. In the simulation project "Ka Maoli Honua" (the Real World Project) developed by teachers at Konawaena Middle School in Kealakekua, Hawai'i, learners take on the roles of adults and immerse themselves in the interdisciplinary project through budgeting household expenses, writing resumes and job applications, applying for auto loans, and arranging childcare. However, one of the most relevant portions of the experience is when students are issued wrenches—unexpected expenses and situations—that challenge students to make decisions impacting their financial stability and success in the project. Students analyze and problem solve circumstances such as unexpected car repairs, unannounced family members moving in, employment layoffs, or health issues that impact the monthly budget. The opportunity to tackle a real world problem—ten with a fake spouse—provides the chance for learners to offer creative and constructive ideas and evaluate the effectiveness of their decision making.

> **Wrench Woes (Activity 16):** The teacher asks students to think about unexpected issues that have affected their own families. The class discusses examples and how best-fit solutions were determined. The teacher explains to learners that they will imagine themselves as employed adults with families and household expenses. Working in groups of 3-4 students, the teams will problem solve how a family would address an unexpected situation—or wrench—without the circumstance completely derailing the family's future plans. Teams will discuss the situation, record a variety of possible solutions and viewpoints, and be prepared to share with the whole class during final discussion. Whether students are participating in the full simulation or not, this activity can be used to support complex thinking.

Supporting complex thinkers is a natural fit for middle level programming. Providing young adolescents with the exposure, opportunities, and resources to stretch their thinking and embrace others' viewpoints aligns with *This We Believe's* essential attributes (NMSA, 2010) of offering developmentally responsive, challenging, empowering, and equitable programming.

Tell Me How, Show Me Now

Target: The goal of this activity is for students to understand how the same image can produce multiple perspectives.

Objectives: (Students will:)

- Use effective communication skills to give instructions for drawing an image or picture
- Work with partners to discuss varying viewpoints for the same object
- Discuss in teams or as a whole class how experiencing other perspectives helps individuals expand their own thinking and understanding

Materials:

- "Tell Me How, Show Me Now" worksheet
- Chart paper and markers

Steps:

1. To link Complex Thinker to the activity, the teacher asks students to share their experiences with multiple perspectives. The class discusses: How can hearing various viewpoints help a situation or decision-making choice? Why is it important to see circumstances through a variety of lenses?
2. Working in partner pairs (trios will not work), students create a barrier with books, binders, or objects. The teacher passes half-sheets out to students with their roles for the activity: Partner One Giver: receives sheet with images; Partner Two Receiver: receives sheet with blank grid.
3. The teacher encourages Partner One's to be as detailed and specific as possible in giving directions and explanations for what the shape looks like, and where it should be placed on Partner Two's grid. Partner Two may ask for clarification, but neither partner may look at the other's sheet.
4. After Partner Two completes all sketches, barriers are removed and both students review the sheets comparing and contrasting similarities and differences of images. Discussion points: How can a shape be perceived differently by viewers? Is there more than one way to describe an object? How does understanding another person's perspective impact your own view of the same situation?

Tell Me How, Show Me Now

Teacher: In order to facilitate this activity, students need to be in partner pairs with a book, binder, or divider between them to prevent visibility. Cut this sheet in half before handing out. Give the Partner One side to the "Giver" role and the Partner Two side to the "Receiver" role. Encourage students to honor the boundaries of the activity to ensure the most authentic experience.

Cut before distributing

Partner One: You will give instructions to your partner without looking at his/her sheet. Be as clear as possible with your descriptions—the goal is for your partner to replicate the shapes from your sheet onto the blank grid.

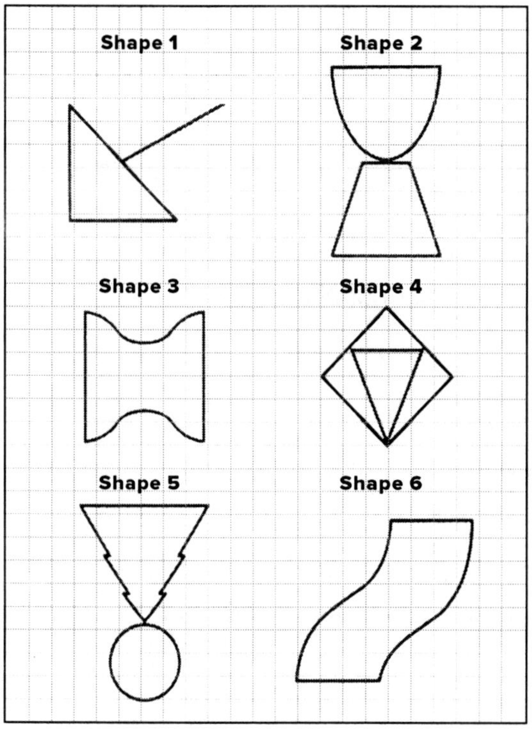

Partner Two: You will listen to your partner and try to replicate the shapes he/she describes onto the blank grid.

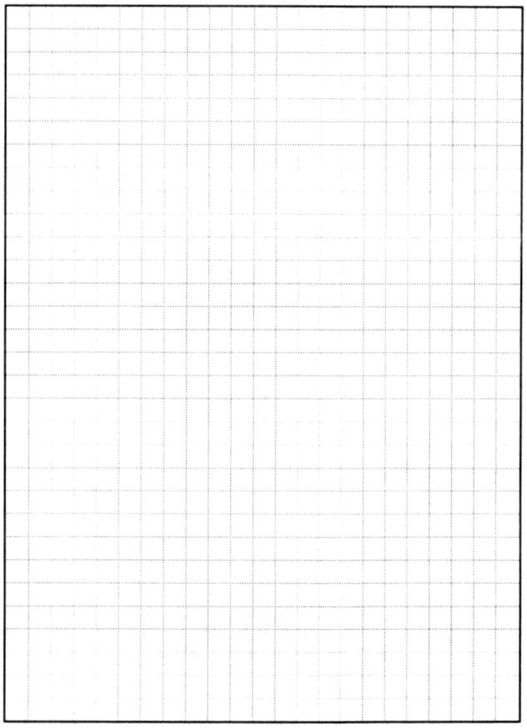

Woulda, Coulda, Shoulda!

Target: The goal of this activity is for students to use problem solving skills to propose solutions to real life scenarios.

Objectives: (Students will:)

- Analyze segments from TV show "What Would You Do?"
- Work in teams to brainstorm and share suggestions for solutions to problems if given scenarios were occurring in their own community
- Share results from teamwork during whole class debriefing

Materials:

- "Woulda, Coulda, Shoulda" worksheet
- Poster paper and markers

Steps:

1. Teacher pre-selects clips from Nickolodeon's *"What Would You Do?"* TV show to share with class. Many clips are posted on YouTube. During the first segment, the class works as a whole group to discuss and debrief the situation. The teacher asks students to contemplate how the scenario would differ if it took place in their own community. Learners reflect and share.
2. Grouping students in teams of 3 or 4, the teacher tells the class they will be watching a second segment and they should view the problem through the lens of their own community. During the viewing, students record notes on the "Woulda, Coulda, Shoulda" worksheet.

   After watching the clip, teams debrief and prepare how they will share suggestions for their own community.

Optional:

- Teams use poster paper during the presentation, combining all members' ideas from individual sheets.
- If computers are available, teams watch different segments of the TV show and each group reports out on a separate topic during whole class discussion.

Worksheet

Name: ______________________________ Date: ________________ Class Period: _____

Woulda, Coulda, Shoulda!

Directions: Based on segments from the show *"What Would You Do?"*, problem solve suggestions your team has for handling the situation in your own town, neighborhood or community.

Summarize the segment viewed:		
How *would* people in this community react to this situation?	What *could* be done to prevent this event in the future?	What *should* be done to educate others about potential harm to the community?

Wrench Woes!

Target: The goal of this activity is for students to use problem solving skills to propose solutions to unexpected real world situations.

Objectives:
(Students will:)

- Discuss responsibilities associated with adulthood in the real world
- Reflect on unexpected situations that have impacted their families
- Brainstorm a list of unexpected problems for which adults have to find solutions

Materials:

- "Wrench Woes" worksheet
- Chart paper and markers

Steps:

1. The teacher asks students to imagine their lives in the future as employed adults with families and household expenses. During discussion, the teacher asks students to share how their current families deal with unexpected situations that disrupt their families' lives. The whole class brainstorms and charts a list of examples (Ex: car repair, emergency room visit, job change or loss, loss of childcare).
2. Working in partner pairs, students select a scenario from the class chart and record ideas, thoughts, and possible solutions to the situation on the "Wrench Woes" worksheet.
3. Partners share results with the whole class and engage in whole class discussion regarding additional suggestions and resolutions to the situation.

Worksheet

Name: ____________________ Date: ____________ Class Period: ______

Wrench Woes!

Summarize the “Wrench” or unexpected expense/situation you are facing:

How will your family’s household budget be impacted by this situation?

What other impacts (not financial) will this situation have on your family?

List all possible solutions to the problem. Place a star (*) next to the one you feel is the most reasonable option. Be prepared to share your choice.

Chapter Eight

The quality of leaders is reflected in the standards they set for themselves.

—Ray Kroc

How to Grow a Quality Producer

Learners who are able to recognize quality performances, understand criteria for excellence, and produce evidence meeting or exceeding standards are destined to be quality producers. To support young adolescents as quality producers, school and classroom structures must include opportunities for learners to use feedback to improve products, processes, and presentations, as well as provide criteria to gauge progress.

Oftentimes, learners believe simply completing a task by an assigned deadline suffices for meeting expectations. Additionally, these same students sometimes resist guidance for multiple revisions of a paper or presentation because they don't understand its rationale. The next activities help students acquire attributes of a quality producer as students generate rubrics and scoring guides, as well as learn to measure their own progress based on feedback and a clear understanding of goals and expectations.

Quality producers learn to integrate goal setting, ongoing revisions, and constructive criticism into planning and practice, as they increase depth of knowledge and skill base through preparation.

Classroom Example

When students define *quality*, they most commonly reference appearance or presentation style. But they often do not mention a connection between quality and goal setting, using multiple drafts, or applying of rubrics. A quick lesson in following instructions helps to debunk the myth of *first-time-is-fine* mantra adopted by so many middle grades learners.

> **Qualities of Quality (Activity 17):** Helps to clarify three key parts of quality: (1) include all parts/pieces, (2) follow instructions, and (3) consider the overall presentation. Students experience the impossibility of creating a quality product when they are challenged to complete a

task without the necessary conditions and information necessary; their frustration with barriers to accomplishing the task effectively helps them see that understanding all requirements and having access to all pertinent information directly impacts producing a quality product.

Community Example

Samples of quality are visible in everyday life from retail displays and media advertising, to public speakers and interactions with employee representatives of business establishments. As concrete thinkers, middle schoolers often assume quality can only apply to tangible or hardcopy examples; whereas, quality comes in all shapes and forms. In fact, an event or experience can be considered of high quality if all plans were executed successfully, or a food server may be referenced as a quality employee based on the interaction and service provided to customers.

Quality merits are subjective depending on the audience, circumstance, and criteria used to measure outcomes. The goal of the next lesson is for students to analyze quality as an idea or concept, as opposed to a checklist or final product.

Quality Events, Experiences and Interactions (Activity 18): After discussing how quality is viewed in the community or through real world activities and events, the class generates a rubric to assess the quality of the event, and, finally, students create their own rubric or scoring guide for an event, activity, or individual's role within the community. They share the final rubrics or scoring guides with classmates and use the feedback to improve their ability to assess quality in everyday situations and interactions in and out of school.

Career Example

Building on Activity 18, students will understand the concept of quality and how it will impact high school years, post-secondary paths, and future real world settings. By using the framework of identifying criteria and setting goals for meeting levels of quality expected, learners are able to better prepare for future opportunities and situations.

The following lesson merges target-setting skills with quality indicators in order for learners to fashion application and behavior toward. When given strong foundations and structural guidance, students are more likely to internalize skills, as well as envision how to use them in future settings.

GLO Setting: How to Set a Personal Goal (Activity 19): Students set goals for their high school, post-secondary, and adult years. To successfully accomplish their objectives, students will identify realistic targets. There is no harm, and indeed, all students should be encouraged to dream big, but lofty or impractical goals such as *I plan to be a millionaire* or *I will star in my own reality show* have sub-goals or more immediate goals that first must be identified and met—and these are the subject of this activity.

Students learn to monitor their progress toward their goals and to communicate with family members to gain additional support. Students may not fully attain many of their goals until they leave middle school; the systems in place help insure students remain aware and attentive to detail as they move forward in life.

Understanding criteria and meeting benchmarks for performance and products are key components to growing quality producers. Mindful consideration of what is expected and understanding how drafts, checklists, rubrics/scoring guides, exemplar models, and goal setting skills are ways learners can be supported in honing necessary skills that will benefit them in the here and now, as well as in the future.

Qualities of Quality

Target: The goal of this activity is for students to reflect on criteria necessary for completing quality work.

Objectives: (Students will:)

- Participate in a "following directions" drawing activity
- Compare and contrast student sample with teacher example
- Discuss criteria and expectations of quality work

Materials:

- Blank white sheets of paper and writing utensils
- Optional: clipboards (if using a carpeted surface)

Steps:

1. Teacher explains that the focus of today's activity is the attributes of quality. Students sit on the floor with sheets of paper placed behind them on floor.
2. The teacher begins reading directions for drawing shapes/objects, instructing students to replicate as much as possible without looking at their own paper or peers' sheets. The teacher completes all directions before allowing students to look at the final drawings.
3. The teacher tells students this assignment will be collected and used for a grade or score as part of their assessment (prepare for panic and outcry). Ask students to explain their frustration and concerns, anticipate reactions such as there was no established criteria, it was difficult to complete with their papers behind their backs, they had no heads-up on grade/score prior to activity. Ask students how they would have changed their final drawing if they had known it would be evaluated.
4. Steer the discussion in the direction of three key components of quality: (1) Does the assignment have all the pieces or parts? (2) Have all instructions been followed? (3) Is the work presentable? Allow students to share other characteristics of quality and how these three key components can help with short-term (daily) tasks as well as long-term (projects) completion. 5) Encourage students to create mini-posters of the "Three Key Components" to hang in the classroom or keep in binders for future reference.

Worksheet

Qualities of Quality

For Teacher Use Only

Steps:

1. Ask students to sit on the floor (if carpeted surface, clipboards may be used)
2. Pass out blank sheets of paper and writing utensils
3. Remind students they may not look at their own paper or peer's sheets
4. Tell students they will draw/replicate the directions you read to the best of their ability
5. Begin reading the instructions
   - draw a square in the center of the page
   - on top of the center square draw a triangle
   - inside of the center square draw one vertical rectangle and two horizontal rectangles
   - outside of the center of the square, on the left draw a tree
   - outside of the center square, on the right side draw two people
   - in the top left corner of the paper draw a sun with a happy face
   - in the top right corner draw some clouds
   - write your name on the bottom of the page
6. After drawings are completed, show students sample (bottom of page) to see how closely their drawings matched. Explain they will be graded on their attempt—be prepared for panic!
7. Use activity to reinforce importance of characteristics of quality: (1) include all parts, (2) follow directions, (3) overall presentation. Use class discussion to reinforce attributes of being a *Quality Producer.*

Sample Drawing

Quality Events, Experiences and Interactions

Target: The goal of this activity is for students to analyze and create learner-generated rubrics for use with events, experiences, or interactions.

Objectives: (Students will:)

- Discuss the attributes and purpose of rubrics and scoring guides
- Discuss how to assess characteristics of quality
- Review a sample rubric or scoring guide for a school event
- Create a rubric or scoring guide for an event, experience, or interaction

Materials:

- "Quality Events, Experiences & Interactions" worksheet
- Chart paper and markers

Steps:

1. The teacher references Activity 17, "Qualities of Quality" (p. 91), highlighting the Key Components as a reminder. The class discusses qualities of events, experiences, or interactions and identifies characteristics that qualify the situation as a quality experience.
2. The teacher distributes the worksheet "Quality Events, Experiences, and Interactions" to students. The class reviews the sample rubric of a school dance and discusses whether the criteria for each category is reasonable for rating a quality experience. Students refer to "Reflective Questions" in order to guide conversations.
3. The class brainstorms events outside of the school arena that can be assessed as quality events, experiences, or interactions. (Ex: community activity, sporting event, customer service, business association).
4. In partners or small groups students select an example from the brainstormed class list to create a rubric or scoring guide of quality for the event. Learners use the worksheet template to draft their ideas, then complete a final version on poster/chart paper to share with whole group.
5. The teacher asks students to reflect on the activity and attributes assigned to each event, experience, or interaction, and to use characteristics in their own situations to demonstrate quality for others to observe.

Name: ____________________ Date: ____________ Class Period: ____

Quality Events, Experiences, and Interactions

Sample: Quality rubric for a school dance

Exceeds Expectations	Meets Expectations	Approaches Expectations	Below Expectations
• Early entry/late pickups allowed • DJ played requests & dedications • Snack bar included pizza • Prom-like decorations used • Admission free for all • All students were well behaved • No waiting lines for entry, restrooms, & snack bar	• Started/ended on time • DJ played requested songs • Snack bar offered variety • Decorations matched theme • Ability to earn free admission • Most students were well behaved • Minimal waiting for entry, restrooms, & snack bar	• Started late or ended early • DJ played same songs • Snack bar needed more choices • Same decorations reused • Admission was same for all • Some students misbehaved • Waiting lines for entry, restrooms, & snack bar	• Did not match posted times • DJ played unfamiliar songs • Snack bar ran out of treats • Minimal decorations • Admission was too high • Discipline issues were obvious • Waited too long for entry, restrooms, & snack bar

Reflective Questions:

- How does the sample above compare/contrast to your own setting? What would you keep/change?
- Which category, "exceeds" or "meets", would you align with quality? Explain.
- Does a rubric/scoring guide guarantee a quality event or experience? Explain.
- How can a rubric/scoring guide assist or hinder planners of an experience or event? Explain.

Worksheet

Name: ______________________ Date: ______________ Class Period: ______

Quality Events, Experiences and Interactions –cont.

Task:

Working with a partner or team, create a rubric for an experience, event, or role that would demonstrate quality. Be prepared to share with the whole class.

Topic: ____

GLO Setting

Target: The goal of this activity is for students to learn how to set a personal goal that can impact their future opportunities.

Objectives:
(Students will:)

- Discuss the attributes and purpose of goal setting
- Discuss how goal attributes need to be specific and measureable
- Review brainstorming list of realistic goals
- Complete a graphic organizer to set targets for goal(s)

Materials:

- "GLO Setting: How to Set a Personal Goal" worksheet
- Chart paper & markers

Steps:

1. Students share with a partner or table team what the purpose of goal setting is. Next, learners brainstorm lists of goals (tried, heard of, aim to set) while the teacher records responses on chart paper. The class assesses which goals from the list are practical and attainable, while eliminating targets considered unrealistic.
2. The teacher offers alternative suggestions if the class brainstorm is incomplete (Ex: read ______ books per ______ ; work cooperatively with teammates; improve speed in track; decrease absences; challenge self to raise hand in class) *Note: Avoid lofty goals such as "become a reality star by age 14" or "retire at 21 as a millionaire."*
3. Based on the class-generated list or their own choices, students plan a goal for a given time frame (week, month, quarter) using the "GLO Setting: How to Set a Personal Goal" worksheet. Steps 1–3 should be completed in class; Step 4 is completed after the goal has been achieved or the time frame for achieving it has lapsed.
4. After students have practiced short-term goals (within the school year), the teacher encourages them to use the same graphic organizer to plan future goals and targets for high school, post-secondary activities, and adult life scenarios.

Worksheet

Name: ______________________ Date: ______________ Class Period: ______

GLO Setting: How to Set a Personal Goal

Step 1: State your goal

____

____

____

____

Step 2: List steps necessary to reach your goal

1. ____
2. ____
3. ____
4. ____
5. ____
6. ____
7. ____

Step 3: Consider roadblocks and obstacles

____

____

____

____

Step 4: Reward and Reflection

How will you celebrate and reflect on the easiest and hardest parts of your goal process?

____

____

____

____

____

Chapter Nine

The real problem is not whether machines think, but whether we do.

—B.F. Skinner

How to Grow an Effective and Ethical User of Technology

With ever-changing influences of devices and web-based information, the field of education is learning to incorporate, model, and evolve for students and educators to progress in tech-savvy environments. Turkle (2011) refers to the *tethered* generation as those who need to connect, or feel linked, to others via technology. Through texting, instant messaging, video chats, social media, blogs, websites and online simulations, students are immersed in each other's lives and have organically invented protocols and expectations to interact through virtual connections.

As with any social contact or working relationship, rules and guidelines help to even the playing field for all involved. Supporting students as *Effective and Ethical Users of Technology (EEUT)* requires the introduction of parameters to reinforce etiquette—or *netiquette*. When learners are transferring digital information or applying technology for personal gain, they must know how to operate efficiently through a set code of conduct.

Effective and ethical users of technology possess the ability to use various technologies to generate new ideas, create projects, access and manage information, and understand the impact technology has on individuals, family members, community, society, and the environment. Additionally, EEUT use technology appropriately for communication, collaboration, research, creativity and problem solving while understanding and respecting the legal and ethical issues aligned with tools, devices, and connections.

Classroom Example

Technology-based interactions capitalize on three of the most common learning styles: visual, auditory, and kinesthetic. This lesson brings the world of podcasts to the classroom by challenging learners to see, hear, and feel information as they interpret the content.

Probing Podcasts (Activity 20): Can be used in any content area and repeated multiple times throughout the semester or school year. The teacher finds a podcast related to theme or course standards to play during class period. Prior to the podcast, students review the worksheet and instructions for *"Probing Podcasts".* After students have gathered information through sight, hearing, and touch, small group discussions will allow students to compare the information that they have collected with that of others.

Community Example

Community can be defined at those sharing a neighborhood, common interest, or regular interaction. In most cases, individuals within a community offer a glimpse of themselves through expression, talent, or skill. A little league team shares the love of a sport while also demonstrating strengths and areas of growth and challenging a competitor for fans to see; political representatives publicly reveal pros and cons for issues involving their constituents; and non-profit organizations fundraise within communities through advertising and media spots. Members of a community expose characteristics and traits based on the level of security shared by colleagues, neighbors, and cohorts. However, when new individuals or participants following different norms join a community, oftentimes perceived safety and security can be compromised. Differing opinions or ideas can upset the proverbial apple cart and a community's mission may need to be revisited.

In the online community of social media, norms are ever-changing, and many times less sophisticated users of technology-based interactions can be confused, led astray, or threatened by unknown persons. The goal of growing effective and ethical users of technology is to prepare students for appropriate behaviors, online expectations, and protective measures to take if necessary.

SpaceBook and Social Media (Activity 21): Drawing on most middle school students' expertise in the area of social media, the lesson invites learners to create faux online personas that can be analyzed, critiqued, and revised for a more user-friendly community connection. Students learn an online community often has limited filters or safe guards, and that not everything an individual thinks, says, or posts is understood or appreciated by the readers. The activity aims to help students see how online communication—taken out of context—can offer a glimpse into an individual's likes, dislikes, activities, interactions, and community status. After the activity, students rethink their own media profiles and online interactions. Recommendations are charted as "Social Media Sharing Dos and Don'ts".

Career Example

Although science hasn't perfected the crystal ball or any other future-seeing devices, humans are forever attempting to look ahead and predict upcoming events.

However, it is hard to believe that a present day 90-year-old who survived the Great Depression would have predicted that transportation would morph from horse and wagon to bullet trains and space shuttles or that communication tools from the 1930s would evolve into real time video chats via handheld devices. What has been accomplished with technology in a century is nothing short of remarkable. It's likely that the current generation's technology will be considered antiquated by descendants of the 21st century within decades.

Students are often asked to envision college or career prospects, family life ideals, and where they might like to live as adults, but few learners are tasked to foresee gadgetry or technology that will improve the quality of life 100 years from now. The next activity brings together creativity and technical insight as students envision their lives complimented by the conveniences of technology.

> **Technology Timeline (Activity 22):** The teacher introduces sample timelines of technology-based items (Ex: telephone, kitchen appliances, automobiles, computers) by referencing the concept of a timeline and how it typically chronicles a person's life. In conjunction with timeline dates, information is shared related to societal activities, science advancement, and the needs of people at each benchmark.
>
> Students are asked to think of a technology-based item from home that has changed in their lifetime— approximately one decade. Students are asked to reflect on the following questions: How will that same item change 10 years from now? Or will it become obsolete? Has it improved the quality of life, if so, how? If not, why is it still available?
>
> To promote cooperative learning, students work collaboratively on a Technology Timeline to show predictions and rationales for three items over the next 100 years. Research, interviews, and critical thinking skills will be applied to the project in order for learners to hypothesize and create educated proposals for the future of technology.

Digital natives are continually moving forward and testing the boundaries of current structures and practices, which means educators and curricular programming must aggressively follow suit. Teachers need to be cognizant of how learners are taught and prepare them with survival skills for the future in order to foster successful citizens (Costa & Kalick, 2010). Instilling effective skills and ethical practices for technological use will help ensure students are equipped with tools and experiences for current and future situations and opportunities.

Probing Podcasts

Target: The goal of this activity is for learners to expand their understanding of podcasts via the senses.

Objectives:
(Students will:)

- Understand the purpose and goals of a podcast
- Review three major senses: visual, auditory, and kinesthetic
- Gather information through senses via a topic-based podcast

Materials:

- "Probing Podcasts" worksheet
- Chart paper and markers

Steps:

1. The teacher begins class by asking students to share the definition and purpose of a podcast. Learners discuss suggestions while the teacher guides the class discussion toward best interpretation (Ex: digital, audio, or video recording). The teacher explains that today's lesson involves listening to an audio podcast and collecting information and data through the use of three senses (visual, auditory, and kinesthetic).
2. Students review the graphic organizer on the "Probing Podcasts" worksheet. While listening to the podcast, they complete sections as information and images are gathered. The teacher encourages students to close their eyes to enhance their experience. The teacher begins the podcast as students record notes and sketches.
3. After the podcast has concluded, student partners or table teams debrief the information and experience. Data can be recorded on chart paper or collected through a whole class discussion.

Worksheet

Name: ______________________________ Date: ______________ Class Period: ______

Title/Topic of Podcast: ____

Probing Podcasts

Directions: Use a variety of senses while listening to the podcast, record responses in corresponding boxes below. Consider closing your eyes for best results. Be prepared to share your observations with partners or teammates.

List interesting information heard.	**Sketch** images seen by the mind's eye.
Describe what you imagine touching or feeling by listening to the narrator/speaker.	What **questions** has this podcast brought to mind?

SpaceBook & Social Media

Target: The goal of this activity is for students to better understand how to interpret communication via social media.

Objectives:
(Students will:)

- Understand the purpose and goals of social media
- Review rules and expectations of online posting to social media sites
- Participate in an online communication simulation

Materials:

- "SpaceBook" worksheet
- Sticky notes
- Chart paper and markers

Steps:

1. The teacher invites students to share their experiences with social media and online communication formats. Discussion points include: pros, cons, and safety advice.
2. Using the "SpaceBook" template, students are asked to create a faux profile based on the characteristics of a middle school student. In the "Recent Activity" section, students show comments or posts from friends or connections to this profile. The teacher encourages creativity and highlights realism. After completing the pages, students hang them around the classroom for a gallery walk activity.

SpaceBook & Social Media–cont.

Steps:

3. Using sticky notes, students draw happy faces, sad faces, or question marks regarding the profiles' posts. The teacher prefaces the activity by explaining an online community often has limited filters or safeguards, and that not everything an individual thinks, says, or posts is understood or appreciated by the readers. The teacher must set up expectations of the gallery walk by stating that the sticky-note commentary is not to be aimed at the author of the SpaceBook page, but rather the focus should be on the sample posts in order to help all students better understand how social media posts can be misinterpreted or misrepresent the author's intent.
4. After class has reviewed most faux profiles, debriefing discussions commence. Beginning with partner pairs, extending to table groups and finally ending with a whole group discussion of Social Media Dos and Don'ts.

SpaceBook

Home **Profile** **Friends** **Inbox**

What's on my mind... **Post**

____
____
____
____
____
____
____

My Stats

Name: ______________________________

Advisory: ______________________________

Birthday: ______________________________

Birth Place: ______________________________

Parents: ______________________________

____

Siblings: ______________________________

____

Pets ______________________________

My Friends

Recent Activity (comments from friends & family)

(about summer) ______________________________
____
____

(about food) ______________________________
____
____

(about movies/TV/music) ______________________________
____
____

(about school) ______________________________
____
____

(any topic of choice) ______________________________
____
____

Photos **Videos** **Contacts**

Technology Timelines

Target: The goal of this activity is for students to use problem solving and prediction skills as they imagine technology's role in their future lives.

Objectives: (Students will:)

- Understand the purpose and components of a timeline
- Reflect on changes in technology of the last decade
- Make predictions for technology use over the next century

Materials:

- "Technology Timelines" worksheet
- Chart paper and markers

Steps:

1. Class discussion focuses on the concept of a timeline and its purpose. The teacher then introduces the topic of technology and asks students to describe how technology has changed over time, along with pros and cons of any modifications.
2. The teacher asks students to think about a commonly used device and how it may have looked and functioned in the past. How might it look and function in the future? The teacher distributes the "Technology Timelines" template to students and explains they will be working with teams to create a poster version of predictions for technology-based items. Categories may include: transportation, communication, and health/safety.
3. Working as teams, students brainstorm items or devices from each category to focus on for the task. Learners research the history of the item to gather baseline data for making accurate predictions. Teams also debate pros and cons of each item and its impact on society as it has changed over the years. Forecasts of each item are made for 25, 50, and 75 years, and descriptions of lasting impacts should also be discussed.
4. Student teams transfer collected information from template sheets onto posters and prepare to share during whole class discussion. The teacher can ask the class to rank likelihood of each items' longevity. Individual reflections can be assessed for effectiveness.

Worksheet

Name: ______________________ Date: ______________ Class Period: ______

Technology Timelines

Directions: Working as a team, develop timelines for the three categories below. Based on research, interviews, and problem solving skills, develop hypotheses and evidence-based predictions for the next 100 years. Use this template as your draft, create a final poster version to be shared with classmates.

	Health/Safety		**Communication**		**Transportation**	
Description of example (present day)						
Pros/Cons of item (present day)	Pro	Con	Pro	Con	Pro	Con
Prediction for item in 25 years						
Prediction for item in 50 years						
Prediction for item in 75 years						
Describe benefits/ detriments (+/-) to society if item lasts	(+)	(-)	(+)	(-)	(+)	(-)

Chapter Ten

All great achievements require time.

—Maya Angelou

GLO-ing Goals and GLO-based Portfolios

Henry David Thoreau stated, "What you get by achieving your goals is not as important as what you become by achieving your goals" (Thoreau, n.d.). The statement reflects an emphasis on process vs. product. This concept is not easily understood by young adolescents who developmentally are ready to become self-reliant in meeting deadlines with work completed for their various classes. Goal setting is difficult at any age, but for middle level learners, the concept can be intimidating if parameters and structures are not put in place to ensure support.

The purpose of goal setting is to establish opportunities for students to identify targets and set reasonable and measurable benchmarks in which progress can be documented throughout the developmental process. It is essential for teachers to convey the purpose clearly and relevantly to students so all students can be successful.

Individuals work toward goals to provide direction and satisfaction in their lives; additionally, they continually identify new goals once they reach their targets in order to grow as productive and contributing members of society (Rottier & Libby, 2005).

Goal setting can be short-term (daily, weekly) for immediate outcomes; or set with long-term (monthly, yearly) results in mind. Goals can focus on various aspects of an individual: physical, intellectual, behavioral, social, or character-based. Regardless of a goal's focus, similar steps are taken to support the process:

Step 1: The student identifies a target or outcome desired by writing it in statement form, such as *I would like to improve my grade in English.* Note the student does not set an extreme goal by expecting to get 100% or straight As, the simple statement of improvement allows for growth and successful results.

Step 2: The learner lists examples of successful activities or strengths that would contribute to this goal *I will write all assignments in my planner on a daily basis; I will review due dates and expectations each night; I will use the rubric and scoring guide to double check work before handing in to teacher.*

Step 3: The student recognizes obstacles that may hinder the progress of a goal, such as I will wait to interact through social media until my assignments are complete; I will increase my homework time from 15 minutes to 60 minutes each night; I will find a quiet place at home to complete my assignments.

Step 4: The learner creates a timeline, calendar, or journal to track progress. The student's own planner can be used and color-coded to indicate tasks completed.

Step 5: The student reflects on completion of the goal by noting accomplishment or obstacles that may have impeded progress. Additional reflection can include identifying successful people in their life and traits that contribute to those individuals' accomplishments.

Figure 1: *Sample Goals for Middle Level Students*

Physical Health	**Intellectual/ Academic**	**Behavioral Issues**	**Social Skills**	**Character-based Traits**
Improve running time/run 1 mile in _____ minutes.	Improve reading fluency/read _____ minutes daily.	Raise my hand to share information/ avoid blurting out answers or questions.	Improve class participation/ ask or answer one question a day in class.	Excuse myself from conversations involving gossip of others.
Increase number of hours of sleep on school nights by 1 hour.	Spend 15 minutes per day memorizing math facts/formulas.	Self-monitor volume level of voice in different environments (class, library, cafeteria, bus).	Make eye contact and demonstrate attentive listening skills with partners.	Invite a new student to eat lunch with me and my friends.
Drink my full 8 oz. water bottle by the end of each school day.	Fill in my student planner daily and check nightly for assignments due.	Follow classroom rules and expectations when a substitute teacher is present.	Volunteer for different roles when participating in group activities/ projects.	Encourage all members of my team to share ideas so no one person dominates the conversation.

Setting and monitoring goals is ongoing in order for students to see value in the process. Daily references and benchmark check-in points reinforce the importance as well as aid learners in understanding necessary steps. Simply setting a goal on Monday and assessing how many participants achieved it on Friday is less likely to yield results, compared to daily status checks with built-in reflection components. Similar to formative assessment practices, goal setting is much more effective when it ebbs and flows with the individual's needs. A summative review of how many goals were set and met is more evaluative and does not encourage or motivate learners to set future goals.

GLO-ing Goals

By using the General Learner Outcomes (GLOs) as a focus for goal-setting, students are reassured that these lifelong learner skills will benefit them in the here and now as well as in future environments. GLOs cater to individualized programming and should be personalized to promote student success. Once learners are familiar with various descriptors aligned to the GLOs, they can identify targets and set objectives with time frames and deadlines.

Figure 2: *Sample GLO Goals*

GLO	Goal Statement	Time Frame
Self-Directed Learner	*I will record class assignments in my student planner and review daily at home to monitor completion status.*	3 weeks
Community Contributor	*I will listen to teammates before offering my opinion in group discussions.*	1 week
Effective Communicator	*I will reread all essays before turning in for evaluation to make sure my message is clear to the reader.*	2 weeks
Complex Thinker	*I will select a topic outside of my comfort zone to complete quarterly project in order to challenge myself.*	8 weeks
Quality Producer	*I will follow all writing process steps and review criteria before submitting final research paper.*	4 weeks
Effective & Ethical User of Technology	*I will record class assignments in my student planner and review daily at home to monitor completion status.*	daily

The GLOs are a support structure for students as they navigate the world of school and real world interactions. Incorporating goal setting into the system allows students to deepen their understanding and practice for overall developmental aptitude.

GLO-ing Portfolios via Student-Led Conferences

Student-led conferences (SLCs) have many forms and functions based on the objectives and goals of each learning environment. Unlike traditional parent-teacher conferences in which only the adults converse and make decisions about a student's academic goals, student-led conferences put the learner in the facilitator's chair and engage all participants to work as a team to support and enhance the student's learning experience during the school year (Kinney, 2012).

SLCs encourage students to accept personal responsibility for their academic performance as well as allow learners to understand the process of self-evaluation. Additionally, the experience helps facilitate the development of students' organizational and oral communication skills, while increasing a learners' self-confidence. Finally, the process encourages students, parents, and advisory teachers to engage in open and honest dialogue regarding learning and academic goals.

Preparation is key for participants of SLCs, as all assume responsibilities for the pace of the conference, contributions through discussion, and support offered to the student for the school year. Based on a 30-minute SLC, the following roles and responsibilities are recommended, as they define what an SLC *Is* and *Is Not* for all involved:

Student-led conferences require coordination on the part of the advisory teacher, but the outcome nets a wealth of information about a student's academic potential, and engages the support of parents and family members for the whole school year. Additionally, learners are more likely to challenge themselves and take risks as critical thinkers when they are empowered to trust the system of support established through the SLC.

Figure 3: *Student-Led Conference (SLC) Roles and Responsibilities*

Student	Advisor	Parent/Family Member
Select artifacts for each section of portfolio Identify strengths and areas of growth for each artifact Review "SLC Is and Is Not" expectations Prepare introduction and talking points for SLC Rehearse agenda by following time limits Determine preliminary goals to share at SLC Complete post-conference reflection	Assist students in aligning artifacts with criteria Assist students with introductions and talking points during SLC Review "SLC Is and Is Not" expectations Review agenda time limits, provide rehearsal time Support students during SLC, but do not facilitate Provide ongoing support to students during SLC and clarification to parents of format Follow up with parents/family members regarding post-conference reflection sheets	Agree to participate in student's SLC; attend at set date and time Review "SLC Is and Is Not" expectations Listen to child explain purpose, artifacts, and goals Hold questions until the end of the presentation; direct toward student, not teacher Refrain from focusing on grades and traditional evaluations –allow student to explain strengths, areas of growth, and goals Share positive insights of child's growth and accomplishments Complete post-conference reflection

Figure 4: *Student-Led Conference (SLC) Formats*

What an SLC *is*...	What an SLC *is not*...	Sample Agenda for a 30-minute SLC
An opportunity for students to facilitate an academic conversation Shared responsibility amongst student, teacher, and parents/family members Review of artifacts arranged in a portfolio by content areas or overarching goals (Ex: GLOs) An opportunity to reflect on accomplishments and set goals for areas of growth A celebration of a student's ownership and investment in his/her learning	Parent-teacher conference or conversation that excludes the student Report card review Identification of only a student's strengths Identification of only a student's weaknesses A punitive event	Introductions and agenda review with purpose and roles (2-3 mins) Explanation of artifacts arranged by content, theme, or overarching goals (15 mins) Goal setting conversation based on strengths and areas of growth (8 mins) Q & A and closure (4-5 mins)

References

Brody Shulkind, S., & Foote, J. (2009). Creating a culture of connectedness through middle school advisory programs. *Middle School Journal, 41*(1), 20-27.

Carnegie Council on Adolescent Development (1989). *Turning points: Preparing American youth for the 21st century.* New York, NY: Carnegie Corporation.

Carruthers, T. (n.d.) Retrieved from http://www.quotegarden.com/teachers.html

CenterSource Systems (2014). *TRIBES learning community.* Retrieved from http://tribes.com

Costa, A.L., & Kalick, B. (2010). It takes some getting used to: Rethinking curriculum for the 21st century. In H. Hayes Jacobs (Ed.), *Curriculum 21: Essential education for a changing world* (pp. 210-226). Alexandria, VA: ASCD.

Erb, T. (2001). *This we believe: And, now we must act.* Westerville, OH: National Middle School Association.

Friedman, T. (2005). *The world is flat: A brief history of the 21st century.* Retrieved from http://www.thomaslfriedman.com/bookshelf/the-world-is-flat

Jackson, A.W., & Davis, G. (2000). *Turning points 2000: Educating adolescents in the 21st century.* New York: Teachers College Press.

King, Jr., M.L. (n.d.) *Martin Luther King, Jr. Quotes.* Retrieved from http://www.brainyquote.com/quotes/authors/m/martin_luther_king_jr.html

Kinney, P. (2012). *Fostering student accountability through student-led conferences.* Westerville, OH: Association for Middle Level Education and National Association of Secondary School Principals.

Kinney, P., Munroe, M.B., & Sessions, P. (2000). *A school-wide approach to student-led conferences: A practitioner's guide.* Westerville, OH: National Middle School Association. Hawai'i State Department of Education (HIDOE, 2013). Learner outcomes. Retrieved from http://www.Hawai'ipublicschools.org/TeachingAndLearning/StudentLearning/LearnerOut comes/Pages/home.aspx

Hawai'i State Department of Education (HIDOE, 2012). *Strategic plan 2011-2018* (2012 update). Retrieved from http://www.Hawai'ipublicschools.org/DOE%20Forms/Advancing%20Education/Strategic Plan.pdf

Kagan, S. (2013). *Kagan publishing and professional development.* Retrieved from http://www.kaganonline.com

National Middle School Association. (1995). *This we believe: Developmentally responsive middle level schools.* Westerville, OH: Author.

National Middle School Association. (2003). *This we believe: Successful schools for young adolescents.* Westerville, OH: Author.

National Middle School Association (2010). *This we believe: Keys to educating young adolescents.* Westerville, OH: Author.

National Middle School Association (2012). *This we believe in action: Implementing successful middle level schools.* Westerville, OH: Author.

Rottier, J, & Libby, K. (2005). *Goal setting for success: Student notebook.* Westerville, OH: National Middle School Association.

Thoreau, H.D. (n.d.). *Henry David Thoreau quotes.* Retrieved from http://www.brainyquote.com/quotes/authors/h/henry_david_thoreau.html

Turkle, S. (2011). *Alone together: Why we expect more from technology and less from each other.* New York: Basic Books.

Wormeli, R. (2001). *Meet me in the middle: Becoming an accomplished middle level teacher.* Portland, ME: Stenhouse.

CPSIA information can be obtained
at www.ICGtesting.com
Printed in the USA
FFOW03n1857310816
27074FF